T0082301

GOING HIGHER
WITH GOD
IN PRAYER

GOING

HIGHER

WITH

GD

IN

PRAYER

CULTIVATING A
LIFELONG DIALOGUE

A.W. TOZER

COMPILED AND EDITED BY JAMES L. SNYDER

BETHANYHOUSE
a division of Baker Publishing Group
Minneapolis, Minnesota

© 2022 by James L. Snyder

Published by Bethany House Publishers
11400 Hampshire Avenue South
Minneapolis, Minnesota 55438
www.bethanyhouse.com

Bethany House Publishers is a division of
Baker Publishing Group, Grand Rapids, Michigan

Printed in the United States of America

All rights reserved. No part of this publication may be reproduced, stored in a retrieval system, or transmitted in any form or by any means—for example, electronic, photocopy, recording—without the prior written permission of the publisher. The only exception is brief quotations in printed reviews.

Library of Congress Cataloging-in-Publication Data
Names: Tozer, A. W. (Aiden Wilson), 1897–1963, author. | Snyder, James L., editor.
Title: Going higher with God in prayer : cultivating a lifelong dialogue / A.W. Tozer, compiled and edited by James L. Snyder.
Description: Minneapolis, Minnesota : Bethany House Publishers, a division of Baker Publishing Group, [2022]
Identifiers: LCCN 2022002390 | ISBN 9780764234040 (trade paperback) | ISBN 9780764240720 (casebound) | ISBN 9781493437382 (ebook)
Subjects: LCSH: Prayer—Christianity. | Spirituality—Christianity.
Classification: LCC BV210.3 .T68 2022 | DDC 248.3/2—dc23/eng/20220210
LC record available at https://lccn.loc.gov/2022002390

Scripture quotations are from the New King James Version®. Copyright © 1982 by Thomas Nelson. Used by permission. All rights reserved.

Cover design by Rob Williams, InsideOut Creative Arts, Inc.

James L. Snyder is represented by The Steve Laube Agency.

Baker Publishing Group publications use paper produced from sustainable forestry practices and post-consumer waste whenever possible.

22 23 24 25 26 27 28   7 6 5 4 3 2 1

Contents

Introduction

You cannot understand A.W. Tozer without understanding his prayer life. Everything he did flowed out of his time in prayer.

One of the many profound things Tozer says about prayer is that we need to "pray our walk and walk our prayer." Sadly, I often find that my own prayer life and walk are completely different. In our prayer, we should begin to bring our life and ministry together and focus on God.

This book is not a textbook on how to pray. There are many of those out there, and Tozer was not interested in that. This is also not a book that outlines an easy method on how we should pray or what the attitude of our prayers should be. No, this book is a direct challenge for you to get on your knees and learn how to pray.

Tozer, throughout his life, got rid of anything that compromised his prayer ministry. His praying was not just a duty he performed to please God, and it was not a ritual he went through to ease his conscience, but it was a ministry. For Tozer, it was his great pleasure to ascend into the mind of God in fellowship.

As I edited this book, I saw that God wants to use me and work through me, and my prayer is the channel through which God can do that. It is like Jacob's ladder: The ladder ascends and it also descends. That means we can go up into the presence of God, and that God can come down into our situation. It is our prayer life that brings the two together.

The most important quote in this book comes from Miguel de Molinos (1628–1696), who said, "Prayer is an ascent or elevation of the mind to God." That is how Tozer viewed his prayer life.

Some things you read here will at first disturb you. That reaction never bothered Dr. Tozer. If you like everything in this book, Dr. Tozer would probably think you have not read it. What he lays out is not compatible with popular culture, or even today's Church culture. Unfortunately, many in the Church today are trying to align their prayer lives with the world around us.

Tozer makes it very clear that God does not hear every prayer. This needs to be grasped by people today, particularly in the Church. The unsaved person has no avenue to God. It is only through Jesus Christ that anybody has access to God. Just because you pray does not mean you have God's ear.

As a Christian, I need to concentrate on discovering God's will on a daily basis and then bring my life into alignment with that will. God makes it very clear that if our prayer is based upon reason or knowledge, it will get us nowhere. God will not be able to work through that prayer.

This material comes from an excellent collection of sermons in which Tozer points out that the greatest curse for the Church today is unanswered prayer. What bothered him most was that most Christians are not bothered by that. Not knowing how to pray is one of the most significant obstacles in our Christian lives, and this book works to overcome that obstacle.

There are many blessings that come with prayer, but also perfect submission. Our prayer lives are a true reflection of our understanding of who we are in Christ, and if Jesus prayed to His Father, "Not as I will, but as You will" (Matthew 26:39), so must we.

This book will help cultivate a desperately needed prayer life, or dialogue with God, in today's Christian. Tozer's challenge to us is this: Are our prayers more powerful and effective today than they were a year ago?

Included is a chapter from the biography of Tozer, *A Man of Prayer*, demonstrating how prayer was the lifeline in all of his ministry and life.

Dr. James L. Snyder

ONE

Discovering the Dynamics of Prayer

Then Jacob awoke from his sleep and said, "Surely the LORD is in this place, and I did not know it."

Genesis 28:16

The most important aspect of the Christian life is prayer. It is the most potent weapon we have in the spiritual warfare before us in this world. Every Christian is defined by their prayer life, and if we are not living in prayer, we are not experiencing the life God has for us.

From the time I became a Christian, I invested my time in prayer. At that time, I didn't know very much about prayer, but through the years I have discovered the marvelous dynamics associated with it. I can relate with what Jacob experienced here.

Every Christian believes in prayer, but few actually live the dynamics of a biblically focused prayer. Prayer is not a ritual or the mumbling of phrases; rather, it is experiencing the awesome presence of God. Out of this presence comes a life of victory and pleasure to Him.

What bothers me is that many Christians do not understand how powerful prayer is and do not take it seriously. Prayer is replaced with works, programs, or methods. They think that if you have the right method, then God will answer your prayer.

But the important thing I have discovered as a Christian is that if I cannot accomplish something through prayer, then it cannot be done by God's grace. The person who discovered this, I believe, was Jacob. But if I could choose between being friends with Jacob or his brother, Esau, I would pick Esau. Esau was a man's man. He was a hunter and was very vigilant in the things he did. He was his father's favorite son.

Jacob, on the other hand, was a momma's boy tied to her apron strings. He didn't seem to have what it took to be the kind of man his brother was. These twins were as opposite as day and night.

One day, Jacob deceived his father and brother, lying and stealing from them, and then he had to get out of town. His mother sent him to her family so he could find a wife there—she did not want him to have a Canaanite as a wife. Because of that, Esau, in defiance of his mother, decided he would have a Canaanite for a wife.

But being a momma's boy, under his mother's instructions, Jacob fled to her brother's place, where he would find a wife to please his mother. When Jacob fled from the wrath of his angry brother, in the howling wilderness wasteland, he saw a ladder standing upon the earth. If Jacob had stayed home in good company, keeping to the house and helping his mother, he would never have seen the ladder. His weakness led to communion with God.

Sin is always wrong, and if we insist on rebellion against God, we will get ourselves into serious trouble. But remember that if you are God's and you belong to Him, you have learned the art of true repentance. God will turn even your defeat into victory. A fleeing Jacob will see a ladder, whereas his brother, Esau, out running around, hunting and bringing in savory meat to please his father, will never see that ladder.

This was an experience with God that Jacob had never thought about before. As he traveled, he became weary, and at the end of the day he grabbed a rock, lay down, and went to sleep. In his sleep, God gave him a dream of angels going up and down the ladder.

The thing I appreciate most about this story is the fact that when Jacob awoke from his sleep, he declared, "Surely the LORD is in this place, and I did not know it." I don't know what kind of a person he was, spiritually speaking, but I think this dream transformed him. He experienced the presence of God, and that would change his life and prepare him for what he would encounter for the rest of his days.

Meditating on the Scripture, I see several important aspects about this ladder of prayer. It ascends, and it descends. This is significant. The going up is an illustration that we have access to God. I do not think Jacob understood this at the time, and even today most Christians don't understand that prayer is, first of all, access to God. It is the key to the treasures of heaven, giving us what God has for us and enabling us to do what He wants us to do.

There is step after step after step; the steps go up and then come down.

In the ascending stairs, we need to understand that the closer we get to God, the farther away we are from the world. This is something many Christians do not understand and have not experienced. From God's perspective, true prayer can never mingle with the world, and the key to this is a complete separation between the world around me and my prayer experience. Jacob learned that if he was going to touch God, he needed to be set apart.

That is exactly what this ladder did. It lifted Jacob out of this world and into the presence of God, introducing him to a world he could never have imagined.

Today, many churches believe that if they adopt the world's business methods, they can build a better church. If you must use business methods or programs to build the church, you have pushed the Holy Spirit to the side. Anybody can build an organization and religion and everything that goes along with that. But only the Holy Spirit can build the Church. And this ascending is the process of separating from the world and focusing entirely on God above.

When Jacob awoke from his sleep, he understood that what he had experienced was something sacred. Once again, we need to understand that prayer is not merely a process or a program, but a sacred and holy activity. We need to grasp the idea that it is communication with God on His terms, not ours. Like Jacob said, "Surely the LORD is in this place, and I did not know it." We can be praying when suddenly we find ourselves going up the ladder, experiencing the presence of God and for the first time seeing that which we did not know was there.

Too many Christians have the idea that they can get away with just adding prayer to their normal daily routines. That is not the truth, but a lie from the enemy. Prayer is not something we add to our life. Rather, it is something we ascend to. The result of true prayer is experiencing the presence of God in reverence and awe on His terms.

If I need to prop up my prayer life with worldly ideas and activities, I do not understand the real essence of prayer. Prayer is discovering the presence of God in a way we did not know before. We cannot truly pray without experiencing God.

Of course, this ladder ascension speaks to the fact that there are various levels of prayer. As I mature in my Christian experience, I am also developing in my prayer ability. My ability to leave the world behind and enter into the presence of God is not something that comes overnight. It's not something that just happens. It is proactive on our part as Christians. We must turn our backs on the world and put our focus on the God of heaven.

Not only did the ladder go up, but it also came down.

The ladder going up means that we can leave the world and enter into the presence of God. The ladder coming down means that God can come down into our presence.

This is not thought of very much. One of the great desires of God is to come down among us. Just as we go up into God's presence, He now wants to come down into ours and fill our lives with the awesome sense of His presence.

That's why Jacob said, "Surely the LORD is in this place, and I did not know it." Once he began to understand and know the presence of God, his life was about to change more than he had ever understood before. The Jacob we come to know after this is the Jacob who experienced God.

My prayer life is not just something I do; rather, it is something I experience. If you would ask anybody, "Do you believe in prayer?" most people would reply, "I sure do believe in prayer." Then if you would ask them, "Have you experienced prayer?" most would look at you with a questioning eye and nod their heads, unsure what you meant.

The problem is most have not experienced prayer the way Jacob experienced it here. Most people go through the motions without the coming down of the presence of God. Prayer is not merely emotional but experiential.

When Jesus was baptized by John the Baptist, a dove came down from heaven and rested upon Him. That was a symbol of the Holy Spirit coming upon the Lord Jesus Christ in preparation for His ministry. We need to have the power and presence of God come upon us as well, and if we do not have this, our Christian experience, especially our prayer lives, will be bland and of no real power.

I want heaven in my life. I want the glory of heaven to shine in me and through me.

Too often, as Christians, we get so caught up with the world that we drag our feet, but what Jacob experienced is what we need to experience. Jacob wasn't the perfect person and still had a ways to go, but he was now going in the right direction.

Christians need to be going in the right direction, and prayer navigates the way forward as we experience the presence of God. His presence is not one-sided, but two-sided. We go up to Him, and He comes down to us. And that interaction is magnificent as we walk in the power of the Holy Spirit.

Most Christians try to deal with the world by accommodating it, making sure the culture is not offended by what they say or do. Therefore, they have ceased to live the radical Christian life of the New Testament. But if I am walking in the power of the Holy Spirit, I am going to offend just about everybody I meet. The reason for this offense is that people have turned their backs on God, which, unfortunately, is even happening in churches today. We have allowed the world, particularly Hollywood, to define Christianity and Christ. I want nothing to do with the Christ of Hollywood.

We need to understand what Jacob experienced when he said, "Surely the LORD is in this place, and I did not know it." When we come to the point of knowing that God is in our place, our lives begin to change.

The most essential thing in my life as a Christian is prayer, but not prayer according to man's understanding. It is prayer in harmony with ascending into the presence of God in such a way that separates us from the world. This prayer experience defines us.

I do not answer to the world. I do not conform to the world. I understand what real prayer is all about and how it separates me. This is the only way I will experience the dynamics of true spiritual separation. I want to examine this as deeply as possible to motivate our hearts to have a passion for prayer as we've never had before.

After Jacob had this dream of the ladder, he said, "How awesome is this place! This is none other than the house of God, and this is the gate of heaven!" (Genesis 28:17).

What Jacob now understood was that prayer is the gateway into heaven. Prayer is the thing that gets us to where God wants us to be so that He can work in our lives as He wants to. I do not tell God what to do. That is a temptation we all have. But I need to get to the point where I am coming up into His presence and allowing Him to come down into my presence at His discretion. And when that happens, I will begin to see things like I never saw them before. I see them from God's perspective.

True prayer cultivates in us sacred reverence and holiness. True prayer gets me to where God wants me to be. It opens up to me all the treasures of heaven I need, to be all that God desires me to be.

We can spend our time in prayer, but it needs to motivate us until we are caught up in the presence of God. Anything less is unworthy of our time.

O God, I long to long for Thee every day of my life. Give me the strength I need to push the world aside so that I can enjoy Your presence in my life. In Jesus' name I pray, amen.

TWO

Barriers to Answered Prayer

Be anxious for nothing, but in everything by prayer and supplication, with thanksgiving, let your requests be made known to God.

Philippians 4:6

When we begin to understand the dynamics of our prayer life, we will appreciate the apostle Paul's words when he says, "in everything by prayer." This was what the Holy Spirit told Paul to write, and what He teaches us today.

I think Jacob understood this when he said, "Surely the LORD is in this place, and I did not know it." Up to this point, Jacob believed he was in charge of his life and didn't need anybody else. However, it was when he discovered the dynamics of prayer that his life changed. He still had a long way to go, but at least he was now heading in the right direction.

I think this experience prepared him for that night of wrestling with God that changed his life forever (Genesis 32:22–32). Jacob had found the answer to dealing with life's problems.

I believe "in everything by prayer" is a remarkable phrase. It is the key to the treasure house of God and confirms that all God has is ours. Unfortunately, Christians are not enjoying all God has for them because they do not know it belongs to them, or because they have not practiced this phrase for themselves.

To realize that God has provided a treasure house and made it available to us is one of the great discoveries of the Christian life. "In everything by prayer" is an unfailing technique for successful prayer and should be on the cornerstone of every church building, in every pulpit, and in every boardroom. In fact, for every boardroom, I would suggest four of these mottos, one for each wall and large enough that no matter which way a board member was looking, they would see it.

I want to explore why prayer is the key to everything we do in God's Church. It is not simply that the Lord said it so now you believe it. There is a reason and a purpose for why He said it that you should understand.

There are two kingdoms: the kingdom of man, and the kingdom of God. These coexist and, to some measure, mingle, but not much. They touch and live side by side with each other, and it is the kingdom of man into which we are born. When the doctor says, "It's a boy" or "It's a girl," we arrive into the kingdom of man, which means we are exiled and in rebellion against God. We are fallen.

We were all born of fallen parents into a fallen society. Members of this fallen race disagree with one another a lot, but they will agree on several things. For example, Herod and Pilate had been enemies but came together when Jesus appeared. On judging Jesus, they became friends again. They were apart in certain political matters but were together on this: They were not going to have anything to do with Him. And so, out in the world, we have the West against the East, race against race, political party against political party, and all sorts of other divisions. But those are just local things. The real battle is God's kingdom versus man's.

Let me lay out here what I believe to be the basic barriers to answered prayer. We have to deal with them or our prayers will never be answered.

The first one is **human self-sufficiency.**

We believe that we are sufficient unto ourselves. Occasionally, you will find someone very distressed, who goes about not thinking much of himself. But if you press him, you learn after a while that he has quite a high opinion of himself and his abilities. And even if he does not have a high opinion of himself, he does have it in humanity and believes in what they call the human race's instinctive wisdom.

The great philosophers talk about the human race's instinctive wisdom, whereas God talks about the human race as prone to folly. God says we are fools, while men say we are wise. God says we act like foolish children and know not as much as an ox. The ox knows his home and understands how to come back to it. In some ways we're not even that wise. A bird knows how to fly home, but we do not know our spiritual home, and we do not know the hand that feeds us; therefore, we are not sufficient unto ourselves.

Some say that if we just cultivate positive thoughts, we can accomplish anything. If that were true, why do we need to be converted? Why do we need the Holy Spirit in our lives daily?

The great blight of the human race is in believing we can make it on our own.

Next, there is the **soundness of moral judgments.**

We believe we know right from wrong. Of course, the human race believes there may be little mistakes here and there—there may be a juvenile delinquent who occasionally shows up—but for the most part, we know what is right and believe in the soundness of our moral judgments.

Everybody means to do good. That seems to be a motto of humanity. Sure, everybody makes mistakes, but nobody should be held accountable for their mistakes since they had good intentions.

Our moral judgments today are based upon a depraved society. All you have to do is read our history and you will find that the decisions of mankind have caused all the pain and agony in our world today. Adam and Eve were perfect people, created by God, and yet their moral judgment failed. We truly cannot tell right from wrong.

Closely related to our belief in the soundness of our judgment is our belief in **human righteousness**. We believe that human beings are right and good as a moral rule.

I, however, believe in the basic wickedness of the human race. That may sound harsh, but unless we understand humanity is evil, we will never strive to solve our problems. Only through Jesus Christ can our problems be solved.

I do not believe in the righteousness of humanity or in the goodness of people, unless God helps us. Unless God gets into us, and unless we get into the kingdom of God, people will not be good. By nature, they are bad.

But apart from Christ, people do not believe this. They cling to the belief that they can become righteous on their own. But the Bible says, "There is none who does good. No, not one."

There's man's kingdom, which is dominated by Satan. It has in it Satan's favor; a history and familiarity and visible success. It is all the flesh, from the flesh, and for the flesh, and dedicated to the flesh into this passing world. Everything about it separates man from the kingdom of God.

The kingdom of man is hopeless apart from Jesus Christ. And as long as humanity believes they can handle everything, it will continue to be hopeless. So where is their prayer, and to whom are they praying?

The success of any church is in its prayer. We can easily deceive ourselves, but purity, power, spirituality, and holiness will parallel our prayer. You could make the kind of graph that businessmen and politicians love so well, with two lines across it. One line would be marked *Prayer*, and the other *Spirituality*, the latter of which would include purity and power and holiness.

You would find that those two lines on the graph might zigzag a little bit, but they would parallel each other almost perfectly. My spirituality is dependent upon whether I do everything by prayer or whether I think I can do it on my own.

Nobody has any scriptural rights to teach a Sunday school class who does not do it by prayer. If he is not a praying man, he will not be a teaching man, because no man can teach something that he is not. They may try to teach the class the truth, but it will not do them any good, and it will not do anybody else any good either.

The teacher always needs to be a praying person. No one ought to seek to counsel others if he is not a praying person. No one ought to serve even in the humblest capacity in any church unless they are a praying person. At least in some degree of regularity, a person who does not practice prayer should never accept a job in any church. Deacons and elders are picked because they are spiritual people, and if they are not praying people, they are not spiritual people. Nobody should ever sit and discuss the church's affairs with a holy body unless he is a praying man.

I am merely preaching a rule that we can see everywhere we look. Wherever the Church of Christ is found, you have to pray or your service will be wood, hay, and stubble.

For our ministry to be successful, we must radically separate ourselves from the kingdom of man. We are not to serve the kingdom of man, but rather we are to serve the kingdom of God. This is difficult for many Christians to grasp.

Serving the kingdom of God means everything we do must be done by prayer. If I am not a praying man, my preaching will not do much good. If I am not a praying man, my writing will not do much good. George Mueller said, "I will not enter the pulpit stale. I will not enter the pulpit dry. If I am to speak anywhere, I wait on God and see to it that the grace of God is flowing in my soul before I dare to address anybody."

Once I discover the dynamics of prayer, it will permeate every aspect of my life. Nothing in my life will have any energy apart from my prayer life. Therefore, I need to deal with every barrier if I am going to keep my prayer life victorious.

I need to recognize that there are barriers, and I need to look at those barriers in my own life and begin to deal with them. I can look at someone else and judge them, but what good does that do?

The most important thing in my life has to be my prayer life; therefore, I will surrender everything in my life to let the dynamics of prayer drive me forward and upward into God's presence.

If we want our church to be a rich, fruitful, God-filled church, we are going to have to accept the Holy Ghost's philosophy "in everything by prayer." We are going to have to accept the Holy Ghost's technique "in everything by prayer." We are going to have to accept it as a rule for everyone from the newest convert to the oldest saint in the church.

"In everything by prayer." I will take this as my motto. I will never try to throw my weight around, but in everything pray, pray, pray that the power of God and the grace of God and the Holy Spirit of God may come upon me in what I am trying to do.

Today, Father, I want to surrender myself and all I do to the activity of prayer in the name of Jesus. I want to evaluate myself and make sure I am not trying to serve Thee in my own strength or by my own wisdom. I surrender completely to Thy authority in my life. Amen.

THREE

The Challenge of Balancing Our Prayer Ministry

Be anxious for nothing, but in everything by prayer and supplication, with thanksgiving, let your requests be made known to God; and the peace of God, which surpasses all understanding, will guard your hearts and minds through Christ Jesus.

Philippians 4:6–7

n the previous chapter, I stated that the kingdom of man into which you and I were born, regardless of our race, is a fallen, hostile, alienated race.

But there is another kingdom, and that is the kingdom of God. That kingdom consists of re-created persons: persons who have been born again, made Christ their Lord and in whom Christ is honored, and have no confidence in fallen humanity. These persons have no confidence in the soundness of man's moral judgments. They believe that left to himself, man will always go the wrong way. They know that they can do nothing in themselves and have no confidence in the flesh, but instead trust in God alone to work in them and through them. These are called Christians, and they make up the true Church of Christ of whatever denomination.

The kingdom of man and the kingdom of God coexist; sometimes they spill over into each other's water and have to be bailed out and separated again. I suppose there is not any church anywhere that is committed to the kingdom of God to the point where God does everything. I believe there will be a little bit of flesh and a little bit of the old Adam in the kingdom regardless of the church. I have never heard of one that did not have a little of it.

But some churches have almost totally given themselves over to the kingdom of man—their philosophy is man's philosophy, their beliefs are man's beliefs, and their viewpoint is man's viewpoint. They go the way man goes and live the way man lives, and yet they call themselves churches.

Then there are other churches in which an effort is made toward making sure that the majority of what they do is divine.

The majority is on the side of the kingdom of God, but around the edges are some things that God is not part of.

The business of ministers, deacons, church members, and Christians everywhere is to make the church as pure as possible. To keep all the kingdom of man out and keep her so replete with the kingdom of God that when you step into the fellowship of the saints, you step into a divine fellowship. The goal is a fellowship dedicated to the proposition that all men are bad until they are made good by the blood of the Lamb, that we are on the wrong road until we find the road home to God through the cross, and that it's only God in us who can do any moral good.

We in the kingdom of God choose for our motto "in everything by prayer," because we have already admitted we cannot do anything on our own. We have already admitted there is nothing in the human muscle that can do the work of God; there is nothing in the human brain that can discern the word of God. We have already admitted there is nothing in human nature good enough to build the holy temple of God. Acknowledging all this, how then can we be pure? Shall we go into a monastery somewhere to hide? No. We are to be active workers, but we are to do this by prayer. Again I say, "In everything by prayer."

Let me point out the contrast between the kingdom of God and the kingdom of man, and then you will see how to locate yourself in the right kingdom.

In Everything by Money

The world says, "In everything by money." Just have enough money and you can do anything. Money talks, opens doors. It's money, money, always money. So the more money, the better things go.

Christ had not a dime and look what He accomplished. But we say if we had more money, we could do a lot more.

The Church, on the other hand, says, "In everything by prayer." We are wise enough to know that money is needed in the kingdom of God, and God uses it and says, "Let everybody lay up in store on the first day of the week." We know that when we give, God takes it, blesses it, spreads it abroad, gives to the poor, and His righteousness remains forever. We know that God uses money in the kingdom of God, but He uses it only because everything is done by prayer. If you have money without prayer, you have a great curse on you.

I believe a curse that could happen to any church would be for someone to donate a hundred thousand dollars, but the Lord not raising up praying people commensurate with it. If God raised up praying men and women with the gift, I would not hesitate to accept the hundred thousand dollars and put it to work. It is amazing what God can do with money, if used prayerfully. The world says, "In everything by money," and then churches rise and are dedicated to the kingdom of man without knowing it. Therefore, they try to run the Church the way man runs the church.

In Everything by Publicity

We need the power of God. Let the public think what they will of us. If we have the power of God and live like Christians, we do not need to care what the world thinks. I want to stand well with God, and if I stand well with God, I am likely to stand well with His best people.

However, some think we ought to have a bureau of public relations. This is how we will build our church.

When first married, my wife and I attended a church until I began my ministry. It was a great church. They prayed and testified and sang, and the power of God was there. At the Communion service, people would kneel and take Communion, and I would see some of them break into tears and laughter along the altar, and the joy of God was in the place. The little church was packed full and we had great times. Then something happened, and there was a tremendous argument among the members—the pastor was voted out and the devil voted in.

To rebuild their church, they established a bureau for public relations, and we used to get literature from them. They grieved the Holy Ghost so He could not bless them, yet they felt they should do something to keep themselves in good with the public.

In Everything by Committee

The Scripture says, "In everything by prayer," not in everything by money, social prestige, publicity, or committees.

Nowadays it seems there is not an hour of the day or night, from spring to the last of winter, when there is not some committee floating around trying to solve problems. We try to do everything by committees. When things go wrong, we get a committee together. "A committee," says Vance Havner, "is a company of the incompetent chosen by the unwilling to do the unnecessary."

We have expensive committees slowing down the work of God. If the Holy Ghost comes on one man, he could make a decision and say, "Open it this way," and bang, it is done. No one has to sit around and talk for hours about titles or about taking a fifteen- or seventeen-minute coffee break.

That said, I am for one committee: I would like to see a committee formed to abolish all committees—for at least a little while. I know you have to have committees. I suppose they are like cleaning the house or scrubbing the dog—you don't like them but you have to do them because they are sometimes necessary. I suppose there must be committees until the end of time. They had them in the Bible and all down the years, and we have them now. But any committee could cut its time in half if it prayed more.

D. L. Moody said that when a man prayed in public, the length of time he prayed was the inverse proportion to the length of time he prayed in private. If he prayed a long time in private, he made his public prayer short, but if he was short in private, he was long in public. I believe that the committee meetings that run endlessly are simply indicating that they have not prayed enough. If we pray more, we talk less.

In Everything by Business Methods

We are trying to do holy work after a modern businessman's technique. It will not work. Once again, Paul said, "In everything by prayer."

Today, when we bring business techniques into the church to deal with the culture, we've got it completely backward. We think that since the culture will have nothing to do with Scripture, we need to develop techniques of the world that will be attractive to the culture around us.

I have nothing against business. On the contrary, we need businesses in our world, and there is nothing better than a good Christian businessman running his company for the glory of Christ. But the church is not a business. The church is not like a grocery store or a lawyer's office or other such ventures.

The uniqueness of the church is that it is empowered by the Holy Spirit. It is a representation of Jesus Christ in this world, and the engine that runs this kind of ministry is prayer. If we engage in prayer the way God wants us to, our churches will grow and expand according to God's expectation, not ours.

In Everything by Education

Some say that what we need is a more educated clergy and more educated ministers. I believe in education; even if you do not get it in school, buy yourself enough good books and get yourself an education.

But when a denomination starts to backslide, I have noticed that they begin to elevate their academic standards. The less we have of the Holy Ghost, the more we have to know about Plato and Aristotle, and we call that being acquainted with contemporary theology. I think we ought to be acquainted with biblical theology: Moses, Isaiah, David, Daniel, Paul, Peter, John, and the rest. But the contemporary fellows kick the theological football around because they are a bunch of self-conscious intellectuals. Nowadays, people talk about neoorthodoxy and neo-evangelicalism. Those are long words and do not mean very much. What matters is what the Holy Ghost says through Scripture.

In Everything by Compromise

In everything by compromise, we try to get along with people. But the Church can never get along with the world. Even when in a position of power, the Church never gets along with the world, and the world never gets along with the Church.

When a politician wants to be elected, he tries to woo the pastor, hoping the pastor will be silly enough to tell the congregation that they should vote for him. I would not vote for anyone who wrote me a letter. Just the fact that he wrote me a letter would be disqualifying; I would not vote for him because he was trying to use the church. The churches ought not to be used; the Church serves our generation by God's will. She will decide how she serves generations; the world will not decide it for her.

The truth is, you cannot delegate prayer. You can delegate some things. My singing, for instance—I can have someone else sing solos for me. But I cannot delegate my prayers. Nobody else can do my praying for me unless I am unconscious. Some people say, "You pray, and we will do the practical things. You pray, and I will sing. You pray, and I will give. You pray, and I will entertain missionaries. You pray, and I will teach, sew, serve." That is a deadly snare.

If you cannot and will not pray, God will not accept your service. If you cannot and will not pray, God will not accept your singing. If you cannot and will not pray, God will not accept your entertaining people. God will not accept your money if you cannot or will not pray. It is prayer that gives power, and all these other things are good things if we set them up by praying. But if we try to do them without praying, we will have wood, hay, and stubble in the day of Jesus Christ.

I surrender all my expectations, O God, and look only to Thee for what I need every day. I pray that my life will be built upon Your expectations and not mine or the world's. Work through me so I will bring glory and honor to Thy name. Amen.

FOUR

The Platform of Effective Prayer

If you ask anything in My name, I will do it.

John 14:14

Here comes the parting of the ways between the man of faith and the man of unfaith. The man of unfaith rejects this teaching flatly: "This is the confidence that we have in Him, that if we ask anything according to His will, He hears us" (1 John 5:14). The man of unfaith says, "That can't be so," and he will not accept it and demands proof from human reason.

Unbelief is a moral thing, not a mental thing at all. Unbelief is always sinful because it presupposes an immoral conviction of the heart before it can exist.

Unfaith is not the failure of the mind to grasp the truth. It is not a bad conclusion drawn from logical premises. It is not the failure or unsoundness of rational reasoning; it is a moral sin. Those of unfaith cannot understand what God's Word says. They can't comprehend the confidence we have in God that He hears us if we ask anything according to His will: "If you ask anything in My name, I will do it." The man of faith feels confident that this is true. The man of faith does not dare let truth rest on human reason.

Someday somebody will try to say, "I have used reason to prove reason is no good." But I'm doing the opposite: I am using reason to show that there are things that reason cannot do.

I have never been against human reason, but I have been against humans trying to use reason to do something that it is not qualified to do. The great difference today in the world is not between the liberal and the fundamentalist, but between the evangelical rationalist and the evangelical mystic—the one who believes in God and disbelieves in human reason versus the one who believes the things of God can be proven by and grasped by human reason. We have evangelical rationalists who insist on reducing everything down to something that can be explained and proven. The result is that we have a rationalized faith and have pulled Almighty God down to the low level of human reason.

Everything was created for a purpose, and I believe there are some things human reason cannot do. Human reason and faith do not lie contrary to one another, but rather one lies above the other.

As believers, we enter another world altogether around what is infinitely above the realm of reason. "My thoughts are not your thoughts, nor are your ways My ways. For as the heavens are higher than the earth, so are My ways higher than your ways, and My thoughts than your thoughts" (Isaiah 55:8–9). Faith never runs contrary to reason; faith simply ignores reason and rises above it. Reason cannot tell us that Jesus Christ should be born of a virgin, but faith knows He was. Reason cannot prove that Jesus took upon himself the form of a man and died bearing the sins of the world, but faith knows that He did. Reason cannot prove that on the third day He rose from the dead, but faith knows that faith itself is an organ of knowledge.

The fundamental rationalists say the human brain alone is an organ of knowledge. They forget there are at least two other organs of knowledge. Feeling is an organ of knowledge too.

All the reason in the world couldn't tell you whether or not you felt hot today. You have your own organ of knowledge: feeling. A young man loves a young woman, yet how does he know it? Does he read the *Encyclopedia Britannica* and reason it out? No. He listens to the ticking of his own heart; he knows it by feeling. Thus, feeling is an organ of knowledge.

Faith is another organ of knowledge. You have to believe certain things. Reason cannot say Jesus rose from the dead. Faith knows He did. Reason cannot say, "He sits at God's right hand, the Father Almighty," for reason doesn't know, but faith knows that He does.

Reason cannot say He shall come to judge the quick and the dead, but faith knows that He'll come. Reason cannot say my sins are all gone, but faith knows they're gone. All down the line, faith is an organ of knowledge. The man who believes has knowledge that the man who merely thinks cannot possibly have. Poor little old brain can come staggering along behind like a little boy trying to keep up with his dad on his short, stubby legs, trying to reason. That's why in the New Testament, the word *wonder* appears—they wondered at Him, and they all marveled. Faith was moving ahead doing wonders, and reason was coming along wide-eyed, marveling; that's always the way it should be.

Nowadays, however, we send reason ahead on his short little legs, and faith never follows. Nobody marvels because we think we can explain the whole business. I claim that a Christian is a miracle, but the moment you can explain a Christian, you have no Christian left anymore.

In William James's book *The Varieties of Religious Experience*, he tried to psychologize the wonders of God working in the human heart. But when the early disciples were on Solomon's front porch in prayer and praise, the people stood back, awestruck, and did not join them. The real Christian is somebody human reason cannot explain, and something psychology cannot explain.

Faith is the highest kind of knowledge, after all. Faith goes straight into the presence of God and behind the veil. Our Lord

Jesus Christ has also gone out for us and engages God Almighty and reaches that for which He was born into the world. He communes with the source of His being and loves the fountain of His life, and He prays to the one who begot Him, knowing the God who made heaven and earth. He may not be an astronomer, but He knows the God who made the stars. He may not be a physicist, but He knows the God who created mathematics. He knows the God of all knowledge, enters and passes the veil into the presence and stands there, touched and wide-eyed, and gazes and gazes and gazes upon the wonders. Faith takes Him there.

Reason cannot disprove anything that faith does; reason never could. Reason supports the Bible by coming to God Almighty's help with a few scientific facts. But all the scientific facts ever assembled in any university of the world could never truly support one spiritual path, because reason and faith occupy two different realms. There are two different worlds—one of reason and one of faith.

If the sun were to start rising in the west and going down in the east, if the summer were not followed by autumn but instead plunged straight into winter, if the corn were to start growing down rather than up, and if the gooney birds were all to start laying eggs and hatching puppies out of them, none of this would change my mind about God or the Bible. My faith in God is not dependent upon the reports of science. They don't know if they've got their science straight in the first place. Faith is an organ of knowledge, and "this is the confidence that we have in Him." Faith mounts upon its long seven-league boots, up toward the mountaintop, up to the shining peak, and says, "God says, and I know it's so."

I do not recommend we have faith in faith. There is an awful lot of that going on these days. People have faith in faith, with men going around preaching faith. No, I do not preach faith, never did, and so help me God, I'll not start now. I know better. Nobody ought to go around preaching faith.

No, we don't have faith in faith; we have faith in God. The Bible says, "This is the confidence that we have in Him" (1 John 5:14). He's the origin and source and foundation and resting place for all our faith. In that kingdom of faith, we are communing now with Him, with God Almighty, the one whose essential nature is holiness. The one who cannot lie, the one before whom go faithfulness and truth. He cannot lie, so we are dealing with a perfect and holy character. Our confidence rises as the character of God becomes greater and more beautiful and more trustworthy.

To sum it all up, my prayer is based upon my confidence in God. Sometimes my prayer seems to be going in the opposite direction of reason. That's a good thing. Reason takes us down the wrong path of prayer, which is probably why many people's prayers are not being answered today.

To pray a reasonable prayer is to go in the wrong direction. Our prayer has to be based upon our faith in God, and that faith is based upon our confidence in Him and who He says He is.

Almighty God, I praise Thy name for the confidence I have in Thee. My desire each day is to build that confidence and to get to know You in such a way that my faith empowers my prayer. Amen.

FIVE

Confidence in Our Prayer

And whatever you ask in My name, that I will do, that the Father may be glorified in the Son. If you ask anything in My name, I will do it.

John 14:13–14

We learn from the promises of God how to pray, but memorizing promises so that we might have *more* faith does not work. I'm a memorizer. I have a copy of the New Testament in cadence form, and the book of Psalms in long-meter form, and I carry them around with me. I am a memorizer and I believe in it.

But if we think that more verses will bring more faith, we're on the wrong track; it won't. Faith does not rest upon promises but upon the character of the one who made the promise. It is written of Abraham that he staggered not at the promises of God through unbelief, but was strong in faith, giving glory to God. The glory went to God, not to the promise. What is the promise for? The promise is that I might know intelligently what the claim is, which direction to go, what God planned for me, and what God will give me. Those are the promises, the intelligent, personal direction God has in mind for me.

The promises are only as good as the character of the one who made the promise.

As I read my Bible, I come across a promise: "This is the confidence that we have in Him, that if we ask anything according to His will, He hears us." And if He hears us, we're promised that God will give us what we're asking for. So how good, then, is this promise? It's as good as the one who made it. How good is that? Faith says, "God is God, the holy God who cannot lie. The God who is infinitely rich and can make good on all His promises. The God who is infinitely honest and has never cheated anybody. The God who is infinitely true and has never told a lie." That's how good the promise is that God makes; it's as good as God is, because God made it.

But often we push God off into a corner and use Him to escape from hell and help us when the baby is sick. Then we go our way and try to pump up faith by reading promises. No, it won't work. We glorify God by putting our faith in God, not the promises. From the promises in the Bible, of course, we learn what God wants to do for us. We learn what to ask for. We learn what God has willed to us. We learn what we can claim as our heritage. We learn from the promises how we should pray. But faith rests upon the character of God alone.

The great God Almighty is not your servant; you're His servant. He is your Father, and you are His child. He has said that in heaven, angels veil their faces before the God who cannot lie.

I think it would be wonderful if every preacher in America would preach about God and nothing else for one solid year. Preach about God, who He is, His attributes, His perfection. Why do we trust Him? Why *should* we trust Him? Why do we love Him? Why *should* we love Him? Keep on preaching God, the triune God, and keep doing it until God fills the whole horizon and the whole world. Faith would spring up like grass at a watercourse. After that, let a man get up and preach a promise, and the whole congregation will say, "I can trust that promise; look who made it."

Confidence may be slow in coming, because we have been brought up in a land of lies. David, in a moment of heat, said, "All men are liars" (Psalm 116:11). But I don't read that he ever changed his mind, even after he cooled off, because everybody is built alike. Everybody has a deceitful heart, desperately wicked by nature, and we are brought up in a world of lies, where lying is a fine art.

We do not have confidence in people; we have a psychology of distrust. If a man comes to my house and offers me a hundred-dollar bill, I wouldn't take it unless I knew the man. But no man can come as a stranger and rap on my door and say, "Pardon me, I am giving one hundred dollars to some upstanding citizen in your neighborhood." I'd say, "You don't even know my name, mister. I've seen your kind before. Good-bye."

We have a psychology of disbelief ground into us from birth. But when we enter the realm of the kingdom of God and the realm of faith, everything changes. Never was there a lie told in heaven; never in the sweet kingdom of God did anybody deceive anybody else.

The Bible tells the truth. It doesn't tell you that you're going to relax and go to bed and sleep twelve hours; it doesn't tell you that you're going to become successful and suddenly grow hair on your bald scalp. It just tells you that you will have eternal life now, with lots of trouble and hardships and thorns and cross-bearing—and glory and eternity with God in the world to come. If you are strong enough to put up with the thorns and the crosses and the hardships and the hostilities, you can have the crown, but you will buy the crown by your blood, sweat, and tears. That is what the Bible tells us.

"In my name," He says. But what does that mean? To ask in His name means to ask according to His will, and this is where the promises come in. You have to understand those promises to know what His will is. Memorize them, learn them, get them in your bloodstream so you will have them on tap at any moment. Purely counting on His merit, the merits of Jesus, that is enough.

We are going to heaven on the merits of another. There is no question about that. We will get in because another one went out. We live because another one died. We will be with God because another one was rejected from the presence of God in the horror and terror of Calvary. We will have the vision beatific because one hung with darkness around Him for six hours of agony. We go to heaven on the merits of another, our faith pressed down upon the character of God and the merits of the Son of God. You do not have to give Him anything, only your poor, miserable soul. The more miserable you feel yourself to be, the nearer to the kingdom you are. As I quoted before, it has been said that humanity is divided into two classes: the good who think they are bad, and the bad who believe they are good.

The bad man who thinks he is good is shut out of God's kingdom forever. But the good man in God's kingdom is not likely to run around talking about how good he is. He is more likely to say that he is not worthy of being called an apostle. He is the chief of sinners and an unworthy servant (2 Corinthians 12:11). God likes to hear that kind of language if it is genuine and truly humble. It relies upon another's merits.

If you pray, "O Lord, I have been a good boy, answer my prayer," you will never get your prayer answered. But if you pray, "O God, for Jesus' sake, do it," you will get your prayer answered. If you come saying, "Lord, if you do this, I promise I'll do such-and-such," you will never get your prayer answered. Throw yourself recklessly upon God, make no reckless promises, but trust His character, trust Him, trust the merits of His Son. You will then have the petition that you ask of Him.

Why can't we see wonders done in this day? I do not believe in wonders that are organized and incorporated. Let others have that. Healing incorporated. Evangelism incorporated. That's not for me. We can have a letterhead, a president, and a secretary and have all that God is not. But the man of faith can go alone into the wilderness and get on his knees and command heaven. God is in there. The man who will dare to stand and let his preaching cost him something, the Christian who puts himself in a place where he must get the answer from God, God's in that. I believe in God, but I'll never be caught asking God to do a wonder just so I have a trinket to play with: "O Lord, do a miracle for me so that I can tell a story." No, no.

God is not going to send Santa Claus toys to His little saints. But if you're in trouble and you have confidence in God, and you go to Him on the merits of His Son and ask Him and claim the promise, God won't let you down. He will help you and get you out of your trouble.

The promises of God, the merits of Jesus' love, and the character of God—these are the grounds on which we base our hope. Not our goodness, not what we promised to do, and not what we have done. If you are in any trouble, why don't you go to God and put Him to the test? Get on your knees and pray it through. Do you have trouble in your home? Trouble in your business? Do you have real trouble? Go to God about it. Get down on your knees, open your Bible, and pray, "God, I hadn't thought about it, but I can trust thee." God Almighty will not let you down.

God will move heaven and earth; He will make the river run backward. He will make the iron swim; He will help out His children.

O Father, we thank Thee for Thy character. We thank Thee for Thy being one God, one majesty. There is no God but Thee, uncreated You. O God, we are blessed.

Now we pray Thee send us out not to be potted house-plants, but soldiers. Let us take advantage of Thy promises; fill our minds with them, carry us back to the God who made them, use us as weapons and tools in Your workhouse.

O God, Satan has laughed at our futile prayers; help us now to go out and make him laugh on the other side of his face.

He's been too long in possession of the field. O God, we claim victory that honors Thee. O God, we want to honor Thee by telling the truth; we want to honor Thee by our prayer. We want to honor Thee by telling all sides of every question, not cheating, not lying, not using advertising techniques to succeed, but telling the old story that others have loved so well and continuing to tell it honestly.

Now, Lord, we are encouraged to believe that what You promise You will do. O God, in Thee we praise and count on the Father through Jesus Christ our Lord. This is the confidence that we have in Thee, that if we ask anything according to Thy will, we will have whatsoever we ask.

In Jesus' name we pray. Amen.

SIX

The Danger of Unanswered Prayer

Whatever you ask in My name, that I will do, that
the Father may be glorified in the Son. If you ask
anything in My name, I will do it.

John 14:13–14

This is the confidence that we have in Him, that if
we ask anything according to His will, He hears
us. And if we know that He hears us, whatever we
ask, we know that we have the petitions that we
have asked of Him.

1 John 5:14–15

You will note the similarity in the language and the phrasing of these two passages, as well as their emotional mood. John was the author of the second one, and he quoted our Lord as having spoken the first one. I want to keep the focus on faith as confidence in God, since this constitutes my philosophy of faith. Evangelicals should dwell on this truth.

John quotes Jesus, saying, "Whatsoever we ask in His name, He will do." In other words, he says we have this assurance that if we ask anything according to His will, He hears us; and if He hears us, we will get what we ask for.

Yet there's a great deal of praying being done that doesn't amount to anything. No good can come from trying to cover this up or attempting to deny it. We would do a lot better by admitting that there are enough prayers any given Sunday to save the whole world, but the world isn't saved. In much of our praying, the only thing that comes back to us is the echo of our voices.

This has a very injurious, sometimes disastrous, effect upon the Church of Christ. Unanswered prayer does significant damage to a congregation over time. It tends to chill and discourage praying people. We become like a petulant child who doesn't expect to get what he asks for but continues to whine for it anyway.

Unanswered prayer destroys expectation. We are tempted to become cold in our hearts and get discouraged. This confirms the natural unbelief of the human heart. Remember, the human heart by nature is filled with unbelief. It was unbelief that led to the first act of disobedience; therefore, not disobedience but unbelief was the first sin, even though disobedience is the first recorded. Behind the disobedience there was the sin of unbelief, or the disobedience would never have taken place. When the Church prays for a sick woman, yet she stays sick or dies, or when the Church prays for deliverance, but never gets it, our natural unbelief is confirmed in our minds. We are tempted to accept unanswered prayer as normal.

Unanswered prayer supports the idea that religion is unreal, that it is subjective with nothing of truth behind it. When I say "horse," everyone's mind immediately jumps to a large animal with short hair, pointy ears, an intelligent face, and four powerful legs. We know what the word *horse* means because it is a reference to something we can see and experience. Similarly, when I use the word *lake*, everybody thinks about a large body of water. I use the word *star*, and everybody thinks of the heavenly body.

But for many people, when I use the words *faith* and *belief* and *God* and *heaven*, there is nothing real behind them. They are just words. They're like pixies and fairies. When we pray and pray and get no answers, we encourage such false ideas in our hearts.

Unanswered prayer gives plenty of occasion to the enemy to blaspheme. The enemy loves blasphemy and is an obscene blasphemer. If he can get Christians howling to the high heaven for weeks on end, and then see that they never get an answer, he has accomplished his goal. Unanswered prayer leaves the enemy in possession of the field.

Unanswered prayer also impedes the development of the work of God. Having prayers sent up to heaven that come back empty is like sending an army out without weapons. It is like sitting down to play the piano without fingers. It is like sending a woodsman into the woods without an ax. It's like sending a farmer into the field without a plow. The work of God stands still.

Jesus said, "Anything you ask in my name, you can have it." And John said, "This is the confidence, the boldness, the assurance we have. . . ." I'm not adding words to Scripture here. Our English language is highly versatile, but the drawback is that sometimes we have to use half a dozen words to mean as much as one word means in another language. When the holy God said, "This is the confidence that we have in Him," that word *confidence* in English is not enough. Some translators say this is the "boldness" we have in Him, and others say this is the "assurance" we have in Him. It takes the words *confidence*, *boldness*, and *assurance* to mean what God meant when He said what we should feel toward Him.

I praise Thee, O God, for the confidence I can have in You and in You alone. I look to the world and become greatly discouraged. I look to Thee and my heart begins to sing with joy unspeakable, full of Your glory. I praise Your name for the prayers You have answered in my life. Thank You. Amen.

SEVEN

Cultivating Anticipatory Prayer

Watch and pray, lest you enter into temptation. The spirit indeed is willing, but the flesh is weak.

Matthew 26:41

The Lord Jesus Christ, the redeemer of men, was about to be betrayed into sinners' hands. He was about to offer His holy soul to be poured out, accepting the accumulated putrefaction and moral filth of the whole of humanity, carrying it to the tree to die there in agony and blood.

Jesus anticipated this crisis and prepared for it by the most effective preparation known in heaven or on earth, namely prayer. Our Lord prayed in the garden. Let us not pity our Lord as some are inclined to do. Let us thank Him that He foresaw the crisis and went to the place of power and the source of energy and got himself ready for that event.

Because He did this, He passed the cosmic crisis triumphantly. I say cosmic crisis because it had to do with more than this world; it had to do with more than the human race. It had to do with the entire cosmos, the whole vast universe, for the Lord was dying that all things might be united in Him, and that the heavens, as well as the earth, might be purged, and that a new heavens and a new earth might be established that could never pass away. All of this rested upon the shoulders of the Son of God that night in the garden. He got ready for this in the most effective way known under the sun, and that is by going to God in prayer.

But over against that were His disciples. They approached the crisis without anticipation; partly they didn't know, partly they didn't care, partly they were too unspiritual to be concerned, and partly they were sleepy. So carelessly, prayerlessly, and sleepily, they allowed themselves to be carried by the rolling of the wheel of time into a crisis so vital, so significant, so portentous that nothing like it has ever happened in the world and never will again.

And the result of their failure to anticipate was that one betrayed our Lord, one denied our Lord, and all forsook our Lord and fled away. Christ had told them, "Watch and pray, lest you enter into temptation. The spirit indeed is willing, but the flesh is weak." These words were precious, like a little diamond set in a ring. But the disciples ignored them to their shame.

I want you to know that the prayer Jesus made that night in the garden was anticipatory prayer; that is, He prayed in anticipation of something He knew was coming in the will of God, and He got ready for it.

This is what I want to emphasize and lay upon your conscience: that you practice anticipatory prayer, because battles are lost before they are fought. You can write that line across your heart and memory, and the history of the world and biography will support it, as battles are always lost before they are fought. It was true long ago, and it is still true of nations today.

Any war that any nation has ever fought was built upon some sort of anticipation, and in that anticipation, preparation. Often the dynamics of that anticipation are not fully known, but the anticipation is important for the success to be realized.

As Christians, we need to understand that we're in a spiritual battle. We need to anticipate a spiritual battle every day. We will not understand ahead of time what that battle is going to be or where it's coming from, but we know of a surety that we're in a war and we need to be prepared for that battle every day. That preparation can only be prayer.

We must understand how to pray for the battle we don't quite understand at the moment. We know something's coming, for history affirms this concept. If I'm going to stand, it will have to be on the Word of God.

The apostle Paul points this out in Ephesians 6:10–18, especially in verses 11 and 12: "Put on the whole armor of God, that you may be able to stand against the wiles of the devil. For we do not wrestle against flesh and blood, but against principalities, against powers, against the rulers of the darkness of this age, against spiritual hosts of wickedness in the heavenly places."

We "put on the whole armor of God" in anticipation of any spiritual battle that comes our way. We must anticipate the battle, and the beginning of this anticipation is prayer. So many Christians are blindsided by a spiritual battle because they did not follow the instructions of Scripture.

This was true of Israel, though on a higher level. In Old Testament times, you will find that Israel never lost a battle when she was righteous and prayed-up. But when she went into a battle filled with iniquity and prayerless, she never won. Israel never lost a battle the day she fought it, and she never won a battle the day she fought it. She always lost her battle when she worshiped the golden calf, or when she sat down to eat and drink and rose up to play, or when she intermarried with the nations, or when she neglected the altar of Jehovah and raised up a heathen altar under some tree; it was then that Israel lost her battle. It was by anticipation, you see, and it was before it happened that she lost.

And this was true of the disciples here, as I've already mentioned. They didn't lose the next morning when one of them cursed and said he was not the disciple, or that night when another one kissed Jesus and said, "Here's the man, take Him." And when even John, who loved Him, forsook Him and fled, and they all sneaked away and melted into the night, that was not when the collapse came. The collapse had started the night before, when tired and weary they lay down and slept instead of listening to the voice of their Savior and staying awake to pray.

If they had stayed awake, prayed alongside Him, heard His groans, and seen His bloody sweat, it might've changed the history of the world, and certainly would have changed their history.

Not only are battles lost before they're fought, but battles are also won before they're fought.

Look at David and Goliath. Everybody knows the story, and we tell it to the children, and the artists paint it. It has a place in the imagination and literature of all the world, how little David with his ruddy cheeks went out and slew the mighty, roaring, breast-beating giant, eleven feet tall and with a sword like a weaver's beam. Tiny, stripling David went out, and with one stone laid him low, and with his great sword, which he could hardly lift, he cut off Goliath's huge head and carried it by the hair and laid it before a shouting, triumphant Israel. When did David win that battle? When did he win that fight? When he walked quietly out to meet that great boasting giant? No. Let somebody else try it, and the words of Goliath would have proved true: "I'll tear you to pieces and feed you to the birds." Under any other circumstances, he would have done just that.

But David was a young man who knew God, and he would slay the giant, the lion, and the bear. He had taken his sheep as the very charge of the Almighty, and he had prayed and meditated and lain under the stars at night and talked to God and learned that when God sends a man, that man can conquer any enemy, no matter how strong. And so it was not that morning on the plain there between the two hills that David won; it was all down the years back to his boyhood when his mother taught him to pray and he learned to know God for himself.

Then there was Jacob. After twenty years, he was to meet his angry brother, who had threatened to kill him. He hadn't seen him in years; he'd gotten away so that Esau couldn't kill him, and now he was coming back. The Lord revealed that the next day they would meet on the plain beyond the River Jabbok. And the next day, they met right on the plain and threw themselves into each other's arms, and Esau forgave Jacob, and Jacob conquered his brother's ire and his murderous intent.

When did he do it? Did he do it that morning when he walked out to meet his brother and crossed over the river? No, he did it the night before when he wrestled alone with his God. It was then he prepared himself to conquer Esau. Esau being the stocky, hairy man of the forest who had solemnly threatened, after an oath, that he would slay Jacob when he found him. How could he cancel that oath? How could he violate the salty oath taken after the manner of the East? God Almighty took it out of his heart when Jacob wrestled alone by the river. Always it's so. Jacob conquered Esau not when they met, but the night before they met.

And so it was with Elijah. Elijah defeated Ahab and Jezebel and all the prophets of Baal and brought victory and revival to Israel. When did he do it? Did he do it that day on Carmel?

Do you know how many words there were in Elijah's prayer? After the prophets of Baal all day long had prayed and leaped on the altar and cut themselves till they were bloody, Elijah walked up at six o'clock in the evening at the time of the sacrifice and prayed a little prayer. Was it a prayer that took him twenty minutes, as we sometimes do in a prayer meeting and shut others out? Was it a long, eloquent prayer? No, it was a blunt, brief little prayer of exactly sixty-six words in English. And I would assume fewer in Hebrew.

Now, did that prayer bring down the fire? Yes and no. Yes, because if it had not been offered, there would have been no fire. No, because if Elijah had not known God all down through the years, and had he not stood before God during the long days and months and years that preceded Carmel, that prayer would have collapsed under its own weight, and they would have torn Elijah to pieces. So it was not on Mount Carmel that Baal was defeated; it was in Mount Gilead, for remember it was from Gilead that Elijah came.

I always feel I'm a better man after reading this story. That great shaggy, hairy man dressed in his simple rustic garb of the peasants came down, boldly staring straight ahead and without any court manners or any knowledge of how to talk or what to do. He walked with his head up, smelling of the mountain and the field, and stood before the shrinking, timid, cowardly, henpecked Ahab, and said, "I'm Elijah. I stand before Jehovah, and I'm just here to tell you there will be no rain until I say so. Good-bye."

That was a dramatic moment, a terrible moment, a wonderful moment, but behind it were long, long years of standing before Jehovah. Elijah did not know he was to be sent to the court of Ahab, but he had anticipated it by many prayers and meditations in the presence of his God.

Forgive me, O Father, for not preparing for the crisis
that is before me. Forgive me for taking for granted
that my prayer is essential to preparing me for what's in
front of me. Thank You for giving me the strength and
the grace to trust You in situations I don't understand.
Praise You, Father, in Jesus' name. Amen.

EIGHT

Prayer in Anticipation of a Crisis

If you faint in the day of adversity, your strength
is small.

Proverbs 24:10

There is always some crisis waiting for us out there. Crises faced Jesus and His disciples and David and Israel and Daniel and Elijah and all the rest. Some crises wait for us today. Let me name a few briefly.

One of them is acute trouble. I hope it doesn't come to you, but the history of the race shows that trouble comes to most of us at some point. And when acute trouble comes with its shocking, weakening sting, some Christians meet it unprepared, and of course they collapse. But is it the trouble that brings the collapse? Yes and no. It is the trouble that brings the collapse in that they wouldn't have collapsed without it. But it is not the trouble that causes them to collapse, because if they had anticipated it and prepared for it, they would have stood tall. "If you faint in the day of adversity, your strength is small."

Your strength is small because your prayers are few and lean, but the one whose prayers are many and strong will not collapse when trouble comes.

A second crisis is temptation. Sometimes temptation comes in a way that is unexpected and subtle, and it's too unexpected and too subtle for the flesh. But anticipatory prayer gets the soul ready for whatever temptation there may be.

Was it the day David walked on the rooftop that he fell into his disgraceful and tragic temptation? No, it was the long gap that historians say came before this when they do not know what David was doing. I know one thing David was not do-ing—he was not waiting on his God. He was not gazing at the stars and saying, "The heavens declare the glory of God," like he used to do. David went down because the whole weight of his wasted weeks bore down upon him. Temptation can't hurt you if you have anticipated it by prayer, and temptation will certainly cause you to fail if you have not.

Then there is the crisis of Satan's attacks; they are rarely anticipated because he is too shrewd to be uniform. If Satan established a pattern of attack, we'd soon catch on to his methods. If he were to be uniform and regular in his attacks, the human race would have found him out a long time ago, and the poorest old church member would have known how to avoid him. But because he is highly irregular and mixes things up, he's deadly if we haven't the shield of faith to protect ourselves.

For instance, take a baseball pitcher: He does not throw the same ball to the same place for nine innings. If he did, the score would be 128 to 0. What does he do? He mixes up his pitches. And the batter never knows where the ball is going to appear; first up, then down, then in, then out, then low, then fast, then down the middle. It is the absence of uniformity that makes the pitcher effective.

Do you think the devil isn't as smart as Dizzy Dean or Billy Pierce? Do you think the devil does not know that the way to win over a Christian is to fool him by irregularity? Never attack him twice in the same way on the same day. Come in from one side one time, then another side like a boxer. Do you think that boxer goes in there and creates an easy-to-recognize pattern? Just lead with his left, strike with his right, move back two steps, and move forward two steps. The commonest stumblebum would win over a fighter like that. No, the fighter has to use his head too. He attacks from one side, then from the other, then dashes in, then backs away, then pedals backward, then charges, and then his left, then right, then feint, then five steps and duck, then weave, then bob, then—you get the idea. And that's the way of the devil as well.

He will come after you today like a wild bull of Bashan, and tomorrow he will be as soft as a lamb, and the next day he won't bother you at all. Then he will fight you three days in a row and leave you alone for three weeks. Remember what was said of Jesus after the three temptations? The devil left Him for a season. Why? To get the Lord to drop His guard, of course. The devil fights like a boxer, pitches like a skilled baseball pitcher, and uses strategy.

And that is why it's pretty hard to anticipate him; you don't know what he's going to do next. But you can always put a blanket anticipation down. You can always figure that the devil's after you, and so by prayer and watching and waiting on God, you can be ready for his coming. And you can win, not on the day he arrives, but the day before he arrives. Not the noon he gets to you, but the morning before the noon.

The only way to win consistently is to keep the blood on the doorposts, keep the cloud and fire over you, keep your fighting clothes on, and never allow the day to creep up on you. Never get up early in the morning and look at your clock and say, "I'll miss my train," and dash away. If you must dash away, take a New Testament along, and instead of reading the *Tribune*, read your New Testament on your way to work. Then bow your head and talk to God. Get ready. I do not recommend this—it's too fast and too uncertain—but rather than not pray at all, grab prayer somewhere in the morning.

God in the Morning

I met God in the morning
When my day was at its best,
And His presence came like sunrise,
Like a glory in my breast.

Ralph Spaulding Cushman

I recommend never letting a day creep up on you. Never let Thursday floor you because you did not pray on Wednesday. Never let Tuesday get you down because you were prayerless on Monday. Never let three o'clock in the afternoon floor you because you did not pray at seven in the morning. See that you're prayed-up ahead of time.

I have some recommendations: Never act as if things are all right. If the devil lets you alone for a while, it may feel as if you're not in much trouble. When you're reasonably happy and reasonably spiritual, you're likely to develop a complex that says *Things are all right*, and you'll neglect your prayer life. You don't watch and pray. Remember, as long as sin and the devil and death are abroad in the land like a virus, like a contagious disease, things are not all right. You're not living in a wholesome world, a helpful world, a world that is geared to keep you spiritually healthy.

> Am I a Soldier of the Cross?
> Are there no foes for me to face?
> Must I not stem the flood?
> Is this vile world a friend to grace,
> To help me on to God?
>
> *Isaac Watts*

So instead of assuming that things are all right, assume they are always wrong, and then prepare for them and anticipate them from whatever direction they come. That's number one.

Second, never trust the devil and think things are all right, because the devil's business is never done. Don't say, "I won't pray today; I'll wait till Wednesday."

Some believe that because the devil may be silent, he has backed away. But we can never underestimate the devil and the trauma that he wants to bring into our lives. The evidence of all of this is a lack of prayer.

Many believe that they have everything in hand and they've got the devil under control, which is playing right into the devil's hands. If the devil can get me to stop praying, I am where he wants me. The thing the devil fears the most about the Christian is prayer. It is prayer that brings the devil's activities down. It is prayer that enables me to win the battle over the devil.

Every day of my life I am in some battle with the devil. If he can distract me, then he can attack me. It is in my prayer life that I truly discern where the enemy will hit me next. That is how I prepare for a battle that I'm really not so sure about. I know it's coming. I know who's behind it. But many times I do not know exactly how the enemy is going to hit me.

Some Christians have come to the conclusion that the devil doesn't even exist. Their prayer life certainly doesn't show much concern about the devil, and neither does their day-by-day living. Because we don't believe it, we have been deceived into becoming vulnerable to those attacks of the enemy.

Always anticipate any possible attack by watching and praying. Never become overconfident for the very reason that our Lord stated, "The spirit is willing, but the flesh is weak" (see Matthew 26:41 and Mark 14:38). Many a man has lost a fight from overconfidence, and many a businessman has lost a business for the same reason.

Never underestimate the power of prayer. "Watch and pray," said Jesus, and He was not talking poetry. "Watch and pray," said Jesus, and He practiced it. He won because He practiced this and caught the spinning world that sin had thrown out of gear, caught it in the web of His own love, and redeemed it by the shedding of His own blood. He did it, I say, because

He prepared himself for that awful event, and that glorious event—by prayer the night before, and by prayer in the mountains at other times, and by prayer down the years from his boyhood.

Remember that without prayer you cannot win, and with it you cannot lose. Granted, of course, that it is true prayer and not just the saying of words. Granted that your life is in harmony with your prayer. But if you pray, you cannot lose. And if you fail to pray, you cannot win. For the Lord gave us the example of anticipatory prayer, getting ready for any event by seeking the face of God in watchful prayer at regular times. Then, no matter what happens, like Jesus Christ our Lord, like Daniel, Elijah, and the rest, you can move triumphantly along, for prayer always wins.

O Father, I refuse to trust my understanding or my wisdom in all things in front of me. I give myself unto Thee and trust Your guidance in my life, realizing that You prepare me for tomorrow. Amen.

NINE

Prayer for the Glory of God

The effective, fervent prayer of a righteous man avails much.

James 5:16

Trrue prayer is not a simple thing. In many ways it is complicated, so many people are not able to figure out the dynamics of their prayer lives. Yes, it is asking and receiving, but it is much more than that.

I want to use three Scriptures that begin to explain the dynamics of our prayer. "The effective, fervent prayer of a righteous man avails much." That is a positive statement. "You ask and do not receive, because you ask amiss, that you may spend it on your pleasures" (James 4:3). That is a negative statement. And finally, "Then He spoke a parable to them, that men always ought to pray and not lose heart" (Luke 18:1). That is a statement of endurance.

The best definition of prayer I have heard is from the great Spanish saint Miguel de Molinos (1628–1696): "Prayer is an ascent or elevation of the mind to God."

Very simply, prayer is an ascent of the mind to God; it is an elevation of the mind. Saying that it is an ascent means that it ascends to God, and saying it is an elevation of the mind indicates there is something you have to do to elevate it. God is above all creatures, and the soul cannot see Him or converse with Him unless you raise yourself above all creatures. So prayer is the elevation of the soul, the flight of the soul, of the mind to God.

The texts I listed above give some specifics about prayer. The first one (James 5:16) says that prayer is a potent thing that avails much, and I would say those words—*avails much* (which means "are effective")—are a terrific understatement. Many do not understand the power that God has invested in this thing we call prayer.

The Old and New Testaments combine to teach and demonstrate how much prayer avails. The Holy Ghost himself labors in this fifth chapter of James to explain this, saying prayer has the ability to turn heaven off and on, causing the clouds to rain or not rain as He pleases.

The second statement (James 4:3) says that sometimes we do not have the advantage of prayer for two possible reasons: either we have failed to ask, or we have asked selfishly, and therefore we do not have the benefits that prayer could bring. Prayer avails much, but we may not be using it properly. When our prayers are simply to satisfy our selfish desires, God will not answer them. Prayer is not for my personal convenience. Prayer is my connection with God on His terms and to accomplish His desires or will.

Then our Lord says in Luke 18:1 that nevertheless, despite the difficulties and problems before us, we always ought to pray. As far as I know, this parable in Luke 18 is the only one that starts by telling what it's going to teach. This is one parable that none of the commentators ever quarrel about. (Often they quarrel about other parables in a good-natured way, disagreeing about what the parable teaches, but Jesus gave them no room to disagree on this one.) We are told, "He spoke a parable to them to this end." In other words, before He told us the parable, He told us what the parable would teach: "The reason I tell you this story is that men ought always to pray and not to faint." He made His statement and then illustrated it with a story.

There is a lot of prayer going on these days. I do not think it would be irreverent to say that God seems to be on everybody's mailing list. Mailing lists are made up of persons who have something the sender of the mail wants. God, who is on everybody's mailing list all over the country and across the globe, is constantly asked for things. But I think that the motive of the asker is usually not any higher than it is when we put someone on our mailing list.

There is a danger that God shall simply be thought of as a great rich man, that He shall buy things for us with His big pocketbook. We aim all our advertising at Him and try to win Him to our side so that we can get something from Him. There is a great danger because every sort of personal and selfish interest these days is being baptized with the waters of prayer. Our prayers may be unscriptural or unspiritual and even downright injurious, and they may have no higher motive than to relieve us from the necessity of earning an honest living or to provide us with something we want.

Many people are praying and boasting about how they are succeeding because they are praying. They run around asking everybody, everywhere, to pray. But it's deceitful. Our prayers are answered according to God's desire. God does not come down to our level as such, but brings us up to His level and uses us through this prayer ministry.

But even if we're not to pray selfishly, that doesn't mean we ignore our own needs. The Lord looks after everything, and the Lord is more concerned about your temperature than your nurse is, and He's more concerned about your health than your doctor, and He's more concerned about your business or your family than you are. So, regarding all the little details we dare to take to God, let nobody tell you they are insignificant. Praying about those things is in the Bible. We can talk to God about the little things, but always remember that these should be talked over with God to seek His will.

There are things we ought to tell only God, which is the significance of prayer. When we pray in private, we ought to pray about private things. And when we pray corporate prayers, we ought to pray about matters that pertain to the corporate body and to the glory of God. If we don't, corporate prayer can be embarrassing and a waste of other people's time. There is a lot of wasted prayer, and I believe the Holy Ghost is displeased because of our so-called prayer requests, which turn out to be personal and private. Sometimes I am afraid we are even praying for selfish things. The Holy Ghost tells us, "Your prayers aren't answered because either you don't ask, you get discouraged and quit asking, or if you do ask, your motives aren't right."

This all boils down to the truth that all our prayers should be for the glory of God and not to glorify ourselves. This is often a difficult discipline for us today. We try to exalt ourselves, thinking that we are making God look good. But the hardest discipline I have in my prayer life is to push myself aside and focus on that which glorifies God.

In order for me to understand how to pray like this, I must get to know God on a personal and intimate level. The more I understand God and know Him intimately, the more I will know how to pray for His glory, and the more my prayers will be glorifying to Him.

O God, Thou art worthy of all glory, and my greatest pleasure is to glorify Thee in all that magnifies Thy name. Help me to discipline myself each day, to lay myself to one side and to focus completely on Thee. May I die to all other things and live exclusively for Your glory. Amen.

TEN

Corporate Prayer: The Blessing of Coming Together

Our Father in heaven,
Hallowed be Your name.
Your kingdom come.
Your will be done
On earth as it is in heaven.

Matthew 6:9–10

Corporate prayer is the body of Christ or Church praying, the people of God praying. And what should be the aim of our prayers? Whatever it is should also be the aim of our lives, so that our prayers and our lives parallel each other. We do not live one way and pray another. We should want something, and then we should live for that thing. So we must pray in harmony with our walk.

A great many people are focused on numbers and are financially successful because they have strong personalities and know skillfully how to take advantage of the public's known habits. Media know how to play with natural human tendencies as well: They know that a beautiful woman or a cute animal or a baby will always capture the public's interest.

Similarly, we know what moves Christians and how they will behave when they're moved. We know the expectation created by the conduct of God's people. Religious leaders learn the habits of the religious public and then play to these habits. Moreover, when they take "bold steps of faith" after praying all night, they are always careful to move in the direction that they know the public has proven they will support.

I do not want anything to do with that. I began preaching on the street corner, and I suppose I can go back to it. We have to *pray* in harmony with high purposes, and we must *work* in harmony with high purposes, and we must *give* in harmony with high purposes.

Now, what are these purposes? There are only two, and from them others may grow. But these two requests or desires should be primary. They should take priority over all other prayer requests, including even the intermittent small prayer requests that I might have about myself and my family.

One of them is the restoration of the most high God's vision for the world. This world should see a vision of the God who would strike them down, a God who would drive them dumb as he drove Daniel dumb or caused John to fall flat on his face. This kind of God is absent from the Church; He is gone not only from liberalism but from the evangelical churches as well.

God's honor has been lost to man, and the God of today's Christianity is a very rich weakling that certain psychological laws can manipulate. That God's glory should return is imperative; the glory should return and be seen among men. We read about it in the Psalms, but we don't know what we're reading. "Be exalted, O God, above the heavens; let Your glory be above all the earth" (Psalm 57:5).

Then we come to the New Testament. "Do this," said Jesus to His Father, "that men may know, and that I have manifested Your name to the men . . ." (John 17:6). He died that God's glory might be manifested to the world, and the coming of Jesus to the world in the first place was so that the world that had lost the vision of God should regain it again.

When the Holy Ghost came at Pentecost, He came to give the heart and the intellect a vision of the glory of God. This is the first of the desires. And I have no hesitation in saying that God's glory should be rediscovered and the world should see what kind of God He is. The Church should once more worship a God whom they respect—the God of the Bible, the God who is the only God. That is more important to God than the salvation of sinners. Now, that may sound terrible, but the Baptists and Presbyterians in other days boldly preached that and did not care what people thought.

But we have gotten into this soft humanism in our time where we weep over rebels and imagine that this is the divine order. That God should be glorified among the nations and His honor revealed to His people—that is more valuable and more desired in heaven among the holy angels and seraphim and all the elders and creatures around the throne than that people should be saved.

But the wonderful part of the story is that the glory of God and the salvation of men have been harmonized in the loving heart of God. God's glory can be revealed as men are converted so that it is not an either/or, something that has to be decided between them, but both can happen at the same time. God will glorify himself by saving men, but He also glorifies himself otherwise.

If we have to choose between the salvation of men and the glory of God, every being in heaven would say, "Thine be the glory." But they would also say that man should be saved.

Now, the first corporate prayer of the New Testament begins, "Our Father." The word *our* makes this a corporate prayer, that is, a prayer of a body of people. And the first request of that corporate body is this: "Hallowed be Your name."

Many Christians fail to notice that the Lord's Prayer was not a prayer for individuals, but for the body to pray together. It is a corporate prayer. It's for all of us in unity. It's designed for the body of Christians to unite in their wants and desires.

The Lord's Prayer starts with a salutation: "Our Father." After that comes the first request: "Hallowed be Your name." In other words, before any other request is made to God, we should want His sacred, holy name to be hallowed before mankind. If we are to follow the teachings of Jesus, then we are to follow this procedure. "Hallowed be Your name." This is first—not second and not third, but first. The glory of God should be restored, and the vision of the most high God should once more appear to men.

If this vision should ever appear to men in churches and be preached again, if the ministers of the sanctuary should go back to preaching on the perfections and attributes and character and being of God, it would soon have the effect of bringing sinners to their knees in confession. It would have the effect of making Christians separate from the world and hating themselves in their carnal ways. They would be like Isaiah when he saw the vision and cried, "I am undone! Because I am a man of unclean lips" (Isaiah 6:5).

John 14:13 quotes Jesus, saying, "Whatever you ask in My name, that I will do, that the Father may be glorified in the Son."

The reason Jesus said "I will do it" was that He might glorify the Father in the doing of it. But Jesus knows, for He says, "That the Father may be glorified is the reason I answer prayer."

No project or organization knows anything valid until God's glory is restored. And in all of our prayers, we ought to pray for this.

The day may come when the people who are now singing over the radio about God and how good He is wouldn't be caught dead singing about God anymore. The people who tasted Christianity will become a disillusioned, bitter, hostile, angry, and cynical crowd.

So the first thing to pray for corporately is the glory of God. The second great desire is that the Church should be delivered from her Babylonian captivity.

This Babylonian captivity has slowly seeped into the American church so that most people cannot differentiate between true biblical Christianity and an impostor. We are being directed away from the true God to serve a false god in all its glory. Most of Babylonian captivity adopts the current culture as the level of worship that it might give. This enslaves us and keeps us from experiencing the spiritual freedoms we have in Christ. We are in bondage, and many do not recognize their own bondage.

It is like the Baal worship in the Old Testament during the time of Elijah. Standing up against this, Elijah worked by God's grace and power to defeat this kind of worship. If my worship today is not based upon my freedom in Christ, I am still in bondage to the Baal captivity syndrome.

We must pray and work that the Church may be freed, that she may come back to separation and devotion and trinity and sanctification; that she may come back again to the glory of God, not in order to be known, publicizing herself, but to make God known. These are the two things that every church is under terrible binding obligation to get done. We need to pray enough and labor enough and live in line with our prayers that God's glory should once again appear among men.

Oh, that God might appear again as He did to the Moravians when God bestowed upon them a loving newness of the Savior. Instantaneously they went out, hardly knowing whether they were on earth or in heaven. This can only come to a Church that takes itself seriously; this can only come to a Church that accepts the truth and will come and yield and settle itself to pray for two things: for the glory of God to be restored and the Church to be purified.

With another generation of decaying rot in our churches, what will we send to the mission fields? We will be sending a defeated, decaying, burnt-out brand of Christianity, which will do the heathen very little good. To prove that this is true, you only have to go to some places now where liberal preachers have been. Some are sociologists instead of preachers, with their gospel of sociology. Go where they have been and you will find Christians that are not Christians at all.

Transplantation of a humanistic sociological Christianity to the foreign field is not fulfilling the biblical text, which says, "Go into all the world and preach the gospel to every creature" (Mark 16:15). The transplantation of publicity, entertainment, and rotten evangelicalism into Borneo or somewhere else is not fulfilling the scriptural directive either. We must take the glory of God and the blood of the Lamb to minority groups hated by the world but loved by God. We must be different and changed and transformed by the glory and the power of God. We must take that kind of gospel to the nations.

If we continue to go downhill in our religious colleges, missionary colleges, and Bible institutes, rotting in decay and tearing apart and pulling away at the seams, the next generation of missionaries won't be worth sending to the field. Oh, that we might have revival that would move us, I as a minister of the sanctuary, and you and all of us, so that there may go out from among us evangelists and missionaries. You cannot be a Bible-believing church and not go out into the world with these two great desires in your mind and heart: the glory of God and the face of Jesus Christ.

Take to the heathen world and to the dying road not only the story that God loves them, but also the story of a great God, high and lifted up, who created the heavens and the earth and before whose face the heavens and the earth will someday flee. A God who in His majesty rides across the heavens, but who also in His love gave His only begotten Son. That's the only kind of gospel worth taking to others. It's the only kind of preaching worth preaching.

Father, we pray that Your glory will be restored and that the Church will be brought out of her Babylonian captivity. Nothing else carries the weight and burden of this prayer. We pray this in Christ's name. Amen.

ELEVEN

The Serpent That Destroys Our Prayer

You do not have because you do not ask. You ask
and do not receive, because you ask amiss, that you
may spend it on your pleasures.

James 4:2–3

The effective, fervent prayer of a righteous man avails
much.

James 5:16

Then He spoke a parable to them, that men always
ought to pray and not lose heart.

Luke 18:1

There is a serpent in the garden still. He wasn't killed after Adam and Eve fell; nobody came with a sword and slew him. The serpent remains in the garden, entwining itself around the loveliest trees and destroying the fruit. Self is the serpent that destroys our prayer so that we may pray and pray and continue to pray without any effect. We may even fast and pray, rise in the night and pray, and still our prayers are not pure, for we're using religion to get something else. Whenever religion becomes a means to something else, and not an end in itself, it is not pure. Whenever the worship of God becomes a means toward something else, it is no longer the worship of God. Whenever prayer and our relationship to God have an ulterior motive, they are no longer pure.

There's much prayer going on today, and people are forming prayer bands and groups everywhere trying to get people to pray. But I am afraid that it can still be said, "You do not have because you do not ask." It can be said, "You ask and do not receive, because you ask amiss, that you may spend it on your pleasures."

Let me show how self entwines itself in our desires, crawls its way through the garden, and spoils even our prayers for us. For instance, we want the glory of God revealed again to this generation, and so carefully we say, "Yes, God, we want men once more to know how great thou art. We want thy sovereign perfection to be displayed throughout all the world, through the sun and the moon and the stars."

We want the glory of God revealed to His Church again, but here's the catch: We want to be the one He uses to reveal it. We want the glory of God revealed, but it has to be through us. We want the veil taken away from the face of God, but we want to be the one who dramatically goes up and pulls the veil aside.

I do not say that all of us do that, but I want to point out here what is often wrong with our prayers and why God has not been able to answer them up until now. If you want to be the one who pulls the veil away and shows the glory of God, then whose glory are you trying to reveal? We want God to reveal His glory but also our own. But God says, "No man shall ever share my glory." God will not give His glory to any other, and therefore we ask and do not receive because we want to spend it on our pleasures.

Similarly, we pray, "O God, deliver thy Church," but we want to be the one to deliver it. Surely God will finally bring us together, but remember the Church is in Babylonian captivity—even the evangelical churches. That is how self destroys our prayers; our motives are carnal, and God has no respect for them. We can call prayer meetings all night or all day, pray for an hour at a time, and still only want to get a bit of glory so that we may share it or God may share it with us. We want the Church to be brought back, but we want to be the ones to lead it.

I want the glory of God to be revealed again to the world, but I do not insist upon being the one to reveal it. So likewise, I want the Church to be brought back from her Babylonian captivity, but I do not insist upon being the one to bring her back.

We want the walls of Jerusalem to be rebuilt. I would like to see the Church of Christ so purified, so filled with the Spirit and His gifts, so lofty in her spiritual standards, so pure and so spiritually cultured that she would recognize a liar when she saw him. She would not listen to gossips or deceivers. If the newspaper says, "This man is a wonderful man of God and preaches in power, so come and hear him," the Church wouldn't listen. She would instantly boycott the whole thing.

That's what I want, but I have to be willing that God should build the walls of Jerusalem without using me as Nehemiah; I have to be perfectly willing that God should take somebody else and let him be the one to build them.

Suppose God said to Nehemiah, "I'm going to build the walls of Jerusalem in answer to your prayer, but I'm not going to use you; you stay behind the scenes and pray." I do not know what Nehemiah would have said, but I suspect it would have been, "Be it unto thy servant even as thou will." If he had not, his prayer would have been for nothing.

God will not answer the prayer of any man, not even to build Jerusalem's walls, if that man insists on building them himself.

We also want the prophets of Baal defeated. There is too much money in our churches—the people with moneymaking decisions that God should make. We would like to see these rich prophets of Baal set back on their haunches and the altar of Jehovah blaze again with the glory of God. We want the theological rodents to run back into their trash cans and hide.

But when we pray, we hope the Lord will use us to chase them out. We want to be the ones to get the stick and start driving out the theological rodents. We want everybody to say, "Ah, that man, isn't he wonderful? He's God's Elijah." So we want Israel brought back from Babylon, but we want to be Israel's leader.

The only kind of praying God will hear is, "O God, bring Israel back from Babylon by whomever thou will."

We must humble ourselves and take the lowly place and say, "Father, use me if you will; I'm before thee. I am like a sword lying here on the table; Lord, pick me up or let me lie. Use me or ignore me. For thy glory, Father, bring back Israel from

Babylon. Build the walls of Jerusalem again. Bring Israel out of Egypt and let somebody else be Moses." I want a reformation. God knows how desperately we need a reformation.

Another error we have slid into in our evangelical churches is that we have become kitchen-oriented. Instead of the cross of Jesus being the center, with all of us gathered around Calvary, praying and fasting, we prefer to minister unto the stomachs of the multitudes.

Whenever you have to gather around the smorgasbord to stay spiritual, you are spiritual no longer; your God is your belly, and your glory is your shame. God knows how far we are away from Him, and how desperately we need a reformation to orient the Church back to the person of Jesus. We are celebrating special days and seasons and weeks—Mother's Day, Father's Day, Kitty's Day, Puppy's Day, and all the rest. We are listening to the world. Martin Luther almost lost his life, and many others did lose theirs, to bring pure Christianity back to the world. We took that holy legacy and stained it.

When we get to glory, we are very likely to meet some anonymous saints who prayed Martin Luther through. He was the warhead in the nose of the missile, and God Almighty used that tough German to do what the weak pastor could not do. Others could not have done what Luther did—they couldn't afford to. They weren't warheads, but Luther was. So God used the man with the hard nose and brought about the Reformation. But I still believe there would not have been any reformation if there hadn't been people, unknown and unheralded, praying him through.

We want the Church to grow, but only if we have a vested interest in it. We want the credit. But do we pray just as much regardless of who gets the glory?

Whenever you want blessings poured into any part of the Church that doesn't involve you, whenever you want blessings for others and anonymity for yourself, your prayers are likely to be pure. If your prayers are for the success of things that revolve around others, they are likely to be pure.

We must elevate our hearts and pray, and here is the praying we have to do: "O God, honor thyself in this fellowship during this week ahead. Honor thyself through me, or ignore me and honor thyself through others. Honor thyself apart from me if it pleases thee. O God, honor thyself, restore thy glory to the Church, but do it in thy way. If that means passing me by, Lord, all right."

God will never elevate you till you humble yourself. That takes a specific type of prayer. A prayer that is fine with God working through you or apart from you. A prayer for God to use you or ignore you. It should make little difference one way or another as long as God works. "O God, reform the Church, but use thine own way of doing it."

You remember Haman in the book of Esther. He wanted honor, but God twisted it around. Finally, the Jew, Mordecai, got the honor, and Haman got the noose. There may be someone else whom God delights to honor, and He may ignore you and overlook you. If you had to take a lowly place among the shadows and your name not be bandied about, would you pray just as earnestly for God's kingdom to come? That God's name might be glorified once more among men and that the Church of Christ might be restored from her Babylonian captivity?

We want a reformation, but we will not insist upon being Luther; let it cost us something not to be heard. We want an army of the Lord to win, but we will stay on the ground and let the generals get the credit. "Lord, we'll live our humble lives, but you'll hear from us."

⁂

When you become a person of prayer, there is a good chance you'll become known as a prayer warrior. And when you come to be known as a prayer warrior, you may be motivated to pray to stay in character, to continue the story others tell about you. A mythology grows up around you that you're a great praying soul. That is dangerous too.

But we can't let that keep us from praying. The Bible says that men always ought to pray. It says that the prayer of a righteous man avails much, and then it gives us illustrations by the dozens from the Bible of prayer that brought down the hailstones, that closed the heavens or made it rain, that made the sun and moon stand still upon Gilboa. God answered the prayers of the people, and we too have got to pray.

The difficulties in prayer that I have placed before you are not difficulties that should stop prayer; they are simply a challenge. You should purify your praying individually, and we should purify our praying as a company of people. God wants people who are unselfish, who want two things above all: that the name of God be glorified in the world and in the Church so that men might tremble at His presence, and that the Church might be restored from her captivity. God's people should not want anybody to get credit except our Lord Jesus Christ.

My criticism is not of those truly seeking to glorify God and restore His Church. I recognize merchants when I see them in the temple. I want to pick them up by the scruff of the neck and throw them out. (Jesus gave us a precedent for doing that.) I wonder how many of us have the proper motivation in prayer.

Too many churches worship a God who is too small. We want the Church restored to the New Testament pattern. We want it so bad that we will pray and work and labor even if it means a loss to us, even if we are overlooked and neglected. God gets all the glory.

I come before You, Father, to humble myself before Thee in such a way that Your glory will be exalted. I lay myself before Thee to be used or not used at Thy discretion. Amen.

TWELVE

Conditions for Answers to Prayer

In this manner, therefore, pray: Our Father in heaven,
hallowed be Your name.

Matthew 6:9

Whatever you ask in My name, that I will do, that
the Father may be glorified in the Son. If you ask
anything in My name, I will do it. . . . If you abide in
Me, and My words abide in you, you will ask what
you desire, and it shall be done for you.

John 14:13–14; 15:7

Prayer changes the individual subjectively and also changes things objectively. I emphasize the former as being more important. It is vastly more important that I should be changed on the inside to suit God than that I should have the power to change an external thing.

The first condition for prayer is that we have a right relationship with God. When you pray, say, "Our Father." But God does not become our Father by our saying "our Father." It is not necessarily true that He was our Father all along and that we did not know it. You may not be one of His children. Jesus was speaking to those who were children of God when He told them to pray "Our Father." God hears His children.

There is a popular notion that God hears everybody. This is not an Old Testament doctrine. The Old Testament Scriptures are very plain that God only heard those who met His terms. This idea is also not a New Testament doctrine. If I want my beliefs to remain in the Word of God, then I must discover whether a thing can be found in either the Old or New Testaments, and this is not. Moreover, Christian testimony, down through the years, has never taught that God hears everyone.

It is a false idea that anybody, anywhere—a gangster on his way out to bump off a rival, or someone ready to rob a bank, or a man whose soul is loaded down with iniquity—can simply pray to the Father, or the "man upstairs," and he will get an answer. This is unenlightened guessing. It is wishful thinking and no more. It has no tradition behind it. It has neither the New Testament nor the Old Testament to back it up. It has not the testimony of those who walk nearest to God.

In 1 John 5:1–9, we have a distinction drawn as fine as a razor blade between those who are children of God and those who are not; those who have life and those who have not life; those who have the witness and those who do not have the witness; those who love God and those who don't; those who keep His commandments and those who do not. There is a line drawn, and you will find that same line drawn through all of the New Testament.

One of the conditions for getting our prayers answered is that we should have a right relationship with God. In Galatians 3:26, it says, "For you are all sons of God through faith in Christ Jesus." These are the ones, and the only ones, who can say, "Our Father in heaven."

Secondly, in 1 John 3:19–22, we read that a good conscience is necessary before praying in order to get our prayers answered. The innocent heart is the confident heart, and the man who has a heart that troubles him, a bad conscience, can never believe. He can pray, and he can pray endlessly, but he will not get anything for his prayers because God will not hear the prayer of one who allows unconfessed sin to dwell in his heart. If he has a bad conscience, the Holy Spirit tells us, there is no use in his praying. But if his conscience is clear, he has confidence in God, and whatever he asks for, he receives.

We must also pray according to God's will. First John 5:14–15 says, "Now this is the confidence that we have in Him, that if we ask anything according to His will, He hears us. And if we know that He hears us, whatever we ask, we know that we have the petitions that we have asked of Him."

God hearing us and answering us are one and the same. One is tantamount to the other and the equivalent of the other. When God hears prayer, He answers it, and we know that we have the petitions that we asked of Him. But we must pray according to the will of God; God hears no prayer contrary to His will.

If people pray selfishly outside of the will of God, there is no possibility of their praying with confidence. They pray without faith. And if they pray without faith, they pray without effectiveness.

There are two ways we can know God's will: by the Scripture —the Word of God—and by the Holy Spirit.

First and foremost is Scripture. We can know that certain things are within the will of God because they are in God's Word, and therefore we can pray within these brackets, knowing that the Word of God gives us full authority to pray for these things. And when the Scripture does not cover certain details, we have the blessed Holy Spirit, who can whisper to our hearts the will of God. These whispers will never be contrary to Scripture, though there may not be a specific text to refer to.

We should always start by using Scripture to pray within the will of God. You cannot know the wisdom of God without appealing to Scripture, and God will answer such prayers and give you the wisdom you need to know His will. There is no use praying outside of the will of God. If you pray within the will of God, He hears you. If He hears you, He answers your prayer. In other words, you should even pray about your prayers to know how God wants you to pray. This has guided me all my Christian life.

Do not expect your prayers to be answered immediately. There are of course some prayers that must be answered immediately or they will not be answered at all. When Peter said,

"Lord, help me!" as he was sinking beneath the waves, he needed an answer right away or there would have been no Peter. They would have had to fish him out and bury him.

But most prayers can be answered over time. Sometimes God allows our prayers to drag along for a while. This is for our good, that we might learn patience and how to trust Him, as well as have the opportunity to be disciplined and chastened and taught. It also gives us time to see if that prayer is of God or not, and whether or not we should continue to pray it.

I believe there are just about as many rituals in the average Protestant church as there are in the Catholic or the Lutheran or other "high" churches. They print prayers and repeat them, and we remember ours and repeat them. There isn't much difference. I could pray a pastoral prayer at nine o'clock any evening, hanging by my toes on a clothesline, and know exactly how to intone it and how to make it work and how to finish it off. It becomes a religious habit. By the grace of God, I want to be delivered from that, even if it means my prayers cannot be beautiful and eloquent. They just have to be blunt praying.

Up until now, my focus has been on having a right relationship with God. You must have a good conscience, and your prayers must be according to God's will and in Jesus' name. But now I want to focus on the amazing promise of John 14:13–14: "Whatever you ask in My name, that I will do, that the Father may be glorified in the Son. If you ask anything in My name, I will do it."

This promise is so overwhelming that you will not believe it, and it is so huge that I scarcely believe it myself. I pray that I might believe it, I try to believe it, and I cry, "O Lord, I believe; help thou my unbelief." Do you know what this verse is saying? God is giving power of attorney to praying people.

Do you know what power of attorney is? You go to a lawyer and sign your name on certain papers to give someone the right to act in your place in anything pertaining to your business. He can commit you to do anything. This scriptural promise gives a Christian power of attorney with God.

Let me put it another way. This promise gives any of God's children the Royal Seal. Back in the old Bible days, they did not have typewriters, telegraphs, TVs, radios, and all the other things we have now. But a man in authority had his seal, a Royal Seal, and that Royal Seal had to be on all documents or they were invalid. Anything sent out from the king that did not bear the Royal Seal got torn to pieces and the messenger was laughed at. But anything that was sent with the Royal Seal instantly had to be done.

Back in the Old Testament, Joseph received the seal from Pharaoh, which meant that anything Joseph did, the king had to back. The Royal Seal was usually worn as a ring—that is where we get our word *signet* ring.

Occasionally, you still see some people with a signet ring with his or her initials cut into it, and that is a hangover from the old days. Instead of having to hunt around for his seal whenever he needed it, a king would wear it on his hand. All he had to do was turn it over and press it into hot wax on a letter, and the letter had the seal.

Jesus Christ puts his Royal Seal on the hands of His people. When the king gave that Royal Seal to someone, that person could go anywhere in the king's domain and act on the king's behalf. He had all the king's authority and the power of the king.

There was not anyone, from the corner policeman to an assistant, who did not hop to attention when anything was spoken in the name of the Royal Seal.

That is exactly what Jesus had in mind when He said, "Anything you ask in My name, I will do it." He was hereby bestowing upon you the Royal Seal. "I put the ring on your finger, and all you have to do is pray and turn it over and stamp the prayer with my name, and it will carry all the power of the King." Your prayer carries royal power with it, absolute authority.

Before I introduced this idea, I said that you would not believe it, and that I myself have difficulty believing it. But it is true. I believe it is true, even though believing it is a difficult thing. Our unbelief tells us that maybe this was true some other time, but not now. Maybe somewhere else, but not here. Maybe for somebody else, but not for me.

But faith says if it happened somewhere else, it is going to happen here. If it happened to other people, it is going to happen for me. If it happened at some other time, it is going to happen now. *O Lord, help our unbelief.* God puts into the hands of His children the Royal Seal.

God is not foolish and will not give the Royal Seal to the wrong person. Never would the King give the Royal Seal to an outlaw. Never would He give the ring to someone He had reason to believe would betray Him. Instead, He gave the Royal Seal only to those who had proved themselves to be worthy of every confidence.

Before Jesus turns the Royal Seal over to His children, He says, "You must have a right relationship with my Father by the new birth, so you can say, 'Our Father in heaven.' You must have a clean conscience. If your conscience is against you, how can you use a holy thing like my name? You must act in my

Father's will, because if you're not in my Father's will, then you are in rebellion, and how could I give a Royal Seal to someone in rebellion?"

Having met these tests, being good children of God with good consciences, living, walking in God's will, and praying in God's will, we have all the authority to move heaven and earth that Jesus Christ has. Do you believe that? That is what the New Testament says. Our wretched unbelief is the reason we do not put it in operation.

Notice the Scripture in Matthew 7:7–8, which says, "Ask, and it will be given to you; seek, and you will find; knock, and it will be opened to you. For everyone who asks receives, and he who seeks finds, and to him who knocks it will be opened."

Even sinners love their children and want to give them everything they want (if it's good for them). How much more will your heavenly Father give good things to those who ask Him? Notice how Matthew 7:11 does not say how much more will your Father who is in heaven give *anything* to those who ask Him.

I would not hand a revolver or a razor blade to a two-year-old child. I wouldn't give a one-pound box of chocolates to an infant. I would want to give *good things* to that child. Only good things are in His will, and the good things are the things you want if you are right with God.

Let's revisit the idea of waiting on God's answer. In Mark 11:22–24, Jesus told His listeners to have faith in God: "For assuredly, I say to you, whoever says to this mountain, 'Be removed and be cast into the sea,' and does not doubt in his heart, but believes that those things he says will be done, he will have whatever he says. Therefore I say to you, whatever things you ask when you pray, believe that you receive them, and you will have them."

I believe that real faith can afford to wait. God's grace often operates through natural events. If you want an ear of corn, plant a grain of corn and wait. Cultivate it and watch it grow. "For the earth yields crops by itself: first the blade, then the head, after that the full grain in the head" (Mark 4:28). That's the way God works. God does not work with slot machines.

I am on a lonely one-man crusade against slot-machine religion. Put a nickel in the slot and get anything you want. That's the way people work, but that is not the way God works.

If God wants chickens, He makes the old hen sit patiently for twenty-one days until an egg hatches. I used to pity hens, having to wait all that time. With some birds, it's twenty-eight days, and with others it's even longer. If God wants an oak tree, it takes Him twenty years to grow it. If He wants wheat, it takes all winter and up to July of the next year. The God of nature is also the God of grace. Therefore, I think we ought not to rush heaven when we pray. We ought to pray in the will of God and then watch God work slowly.

I have asked God for things and almost gotten discouraged, and then finally saw them begin to happen. Americans have brass knockers, and they knock three times and want to go right in. The kingdom of heaven can wait, and you can wait, and I can wait. Let us trust God and be patient. Some people in the Old Testament—even in the eleventh chapter of Hebrews, the Westminster Abbey of the Bible—died before their prayers were answered.

I pray to Thee, O heavenly Father, that I will patiently wait on Thee for the answer to my prayers. I will search Thy Word to make sure I am praying within the confines of Thy will. Bless Thou my prayers today, in Jesus' name. Amen.

THIRTEEN

How to Pray Successfully

You ask and do not receive, because you ask amiss, that you may spend it on your pleasures.

James 4:3

f you want to pray successfully—and I take it you do—your whole life has to pray. Praying only at the last minute when you're in an emergency is not what God wants.

God sometimes answers emergency prayers. There is not any doubt about that. Often people ask if God hears scared prayers. He does hear the prayers of His true people no matter what, which means He hears our emergency prayers.

I will not tell you that your life must be perfect before God hears your prayers, but I will tell you that while God does turn aside and sometimes hear emergency prayers, that is not His highest will. His highest will is that we should live the way we pray.

In his most famous book, *A Serious Call to Religion*, William Law makes an argument that I read twenty-five years ago, and it has stuck with me ever since. He says our trouble is often that we pray one way and walk another, and thus we cross ourselves up. Therefore, he said, we ought to go the way we pray. Our prayer ought to go the way our life is going. The man who walks a holy walk can pray a holy prayer, but if he tries to pray a holy prayer and walk an unholy life, he is crossing himself up. So he pleads that the people of God might begin to live the way they pray. That is what I mean here.

Our whole life ought to pray. By that I mean our whole life should be a prayer, a sacrifice on the altar. There should be nothing in my life that can cancel out my prayers. There should be nothing in my conduct, thoughts, deeds, ambitions, or relationships with people that could make it impossible for God to answer my prayer.

I think the greatest prayer in the world is the unuttered prayer of a great life. Jesus prayed consistently. He prayed long prayers.

He prayed before meals. He prayed in company. He prayed with others. He prayed alone. He prayed every kind of prayer I suppose there was. But the greatest prayer He ever made was the walk He took from the time He toddled out of Joseph's carpenter shop until they nailed Him on a cross. His life was His greatest prayer.

The Bible says Jesus pleads for us at the right hand of God the Father Almighty, making intercession for us continually. That has given some people the impression that Jesus Christ is engaging in perpetual prayer, meeting on His knees before the Father, interceding forever. No, His presence there is the most eloquent prayer in all the universe. He is there before God, wearing our nature and our shape and looking like us. An angel walking in heaven could see that form and say that a man has arrived. A man is in heaven. Our man. God's man. The sample man. The second Adam. His presence there at the right hand of God is a great eloquent prayer for you and me. He bears our names on His hands, His shoulders, and His breast. There before the Father, His eloquent presence is His mighty efficacious prayer.

Similarly, I believe the greatest prayer in the world is the prayer of the life that is moving in the right direction. I don't want to "spiritualize" praying so it loses its meaning, or give it a mystical turn and relieve us of the privilege and necessity of praying for specific things and expecting them. Let us do that too. But I think a person will be mighty unskillful in prayer if he has to wash up, get a quick haircut, and straighten himself out when he walks into the presence of God. He should have been like that all the time. A man who allows himself four days' growth of beard and clothes that are soiled, and then suddenly has to appear before the King, has to do some fast footwork to get ready for that royal appearance. But he should be prepared at all times. I mean that morally, of course. God doesn't need you to dress up for Him. God's people should never need to morally and spiritually rush around and get straightened up to get into the presence of their King. They should live so that they can enter that presence at any time without embarrassment. They should have on the proper robes to go into His presence.

James 4:2–3 says, "You do not have because you do not ask. You ask and do not receive, because you ask amiss, that you may spend it on your pleasures." In John 16:24, Jesus says, "Ask, and you will receive."

Here we have the word *ask* four times. You have not because you ask not, and having not is the penalty of prayerlessness. You could have what you want or need if you had only asked for it. You are not asking for it, so you are not getting it. How little we have may be the result of how little we ask.

But the verse also says that "you ask and do not receive, because you ask amiss, that you may spend it on your pleasures." That is the penalty of selfishness. Asking selfishly that I might have it to spend it on my pleasures—or put another way, with the wrong motives—will make it impossible for God to answer.

Yet if you ask with the right motives, you shall receive. That is the reward of faithfulness. *He has not because he asks not* is the penalty of prayerlessness.

I hope this has encouraged you to know that prayer is not simply something religious-minded people mumble, but that it is a science, an art, and a skill all to be learned by God's grace. It is a privilege to be enjoyed, an authority to be wielded, for these are the rights you and I have in the Lamb. We can go to God and ask what we will and it shall be done unto us. Do you believe that? Will you then practice it more than you have been? Would you pray fifteen minutes more a day than you have been praying? Will you take this upon yourself? Will you dare to go to God?

Wishing, on the other hand, is not the same as praying. We need to stop wishing when we should be praying. God's poor sheep are always wishing, wishing, wishing. We're like a farmer who sits on the front porch and wishes for ten acres of golden corn. He calls his wife and says, "Mary, would you please join me in wishing for ten acres of golden corn?" So she joins him. She says to him, "George, I think that we ought to call in our neighbors. I think there is power in numbers. Let's call in our neighbors." So she goes to the phone, rings three times, and when the neighbor answers, she says, "Come on over. George and I are sitting on the front porch, wishing for ten acres of golden corn." She is going to have her porch full of people, all sitting there wishing for corn.

I know that is ridiculous, but a lot of God's children are doing the same thing. They wish for things. Stop wishing. If you ought to have it, pray and you will get it. If you can get it without asking for it by a miracle, get it. Go do it. God will not do what you can do, and there is no use trying to do what only God can do. We can get tangled up trying to do for ourselves what only God can do, and asking God to do what we can do ourselves.

I remember an old story of D. L. Moody. He came into a prayer meeting one time where there were a lot of moneyed men—Christian men of wealth. As he walked in, all he saw were the soles of a whole lot of businessmen's shoes around the circle, and they were asking God for fifteen hundred dollars. The little blunt Moody said, "Brethren, get up. I don't think I'd bother God any more about that." He told them that any of them could have written a check and never noticed it was gone from their account. They were down on their knees, asking God Almighty to give them what they could have gotten by a scratch of the pen. Don't waste your time asking for things you can do yourself. Just do them.

God is not going to spoil us by waiting on us hand and foot. God will not make your bed. God will not wash your dishes. God will not mow your lawn. God will not shovel your snow.

If you can do it, do it. Do not bother God about it. There are so many things you cannot do, and those are the things God wants to do for you.

God specializes in the impossible. With God, all things are possible, and all things are possible to him that believes. There is a realm of impossibilities, a realm of exploits where human brains and human hands cannot do; only God Almighty can. That is where prayer becomes powerful. Prayer moves the hand that moves nature in the world. If you can do it, do it. If God does not want you to have it, do not waste your time wishing for it; you'll only learn bad mental habits. If God does not want you to have it, do not want it. If He wants you to have it and you cannot get it honestly, pray for it—that is, if it is within His will, if it is unselfish, if it is for His glory, and if it is for the good of humanity. If all these things are so, then pray for it, and the Lord will answer your prayers.

You have the Royal Seal. I hope you will learn how to use it. What could we do if we learned to use the authority given to us by our Savior? We are deliberately not using man's methods in the Church. We have repudiated them as bad opportunism and advertising methods. We are trying to do things the New Testament way. But look out, because if we choose the New

Testament way, then we must have the New Testament spirit. To take the New Testament way and then not live the New Testament life would be acting against ourselves.

Let us believe God together, and let us pray more than we have been. You have not because you ask not. Put prayer to work. See what God will do for you and your family, for your business, home, church, life, and country. Everywhere within the will of God, green grass will spring up by the watercourses, and where dragons used to lie, roses shall bloom. You will find yourself wonderfully enriched as you pray, believing.

Heavenly Father, we thank Thee for the privilege of prayer. We thank Thee that we are not out of touch with heaven. We thank Thee that You incline Your ear unto us and hear us. We confess to Thee our staggering unbelief and our doubting. We confess to Thee, Lord, that as a company, we have not dared to be as bold as we should, but we want to correct that. We want to dare to come boldly to the throne of grace and ask for what we need. Thank You for the answers we have seen, marvelous answers, Lord, which could not have come except that You sent them.

But there are still some things unanswered. O Lord, we pray Thou make this a praying church. Make these people so bold, so aggressive in their praying that they will cry unto Thee and dare to continue to pray until the answer arrives, even if it takes weeks, months, and in some instances, maybe years, but answers will come with our God. Teach us to pray, O Lord; teach us to pray in Jesus' name. Amen.

FOURTEEN

Things Prayer Will Do for You

In that day you will ask in My name, and I do not say to you that I shall pray the Father for you; for the Father Himself loves you, because you have loved Me, and have believed that I came forth from God.

John 16:26–27

Whatever you ask in My name, that I will do, that the Father may be glorified in the Son. If you ask anything in My name, I will do it.

John 14:13–14

If you abide in Me, and My words abide in you, you will ask what you desire, and it shall be done for you.

John 15:7

want to sketch briefly in this chapter the things prayer will do for us and what we may expect God to do in answer to prayer.

There are seven provinces of prayer, and any one of these would be well worthy of a full chapter. The provinces are our personal spiritual lives, our bodies, our families, our material needs, our friends, our country, and the progress of the gospel. In this chapter, the progress of the gospel will receive the greatest emphasis.

But first a note about God's involvement in every aspect of our lives. Some say there is no use talking to God about any of these things, that it is impossible to believe that a God as great as the God who speaks in thunder, the Almighty God who holds the world in His hand, should be interested in such details. They conceive God to be the chairman of the board or the president of a vast company. Asking the company president to replenish the paper cups in the dispensary at the water cooler is akin to asking the most high God to be interested in any of the small details of our lives.

But if there is anything the Incarnation of Jesus accomplished, it was to destroy this idea of a God too big for details. When Jesus Christ, the eternal Son, before He was incarnated, left heaven and came down in the form of a man and took upon himself our nature and our flesh, He became one of us. One, that is, without our sin nature. From this we must conclude that God is interested in us in detail, that God is not the president of a company far removed from the workers or the top figure in a descending scale of other important figures. God, being who He is, can take care of the sparrow, the grass, and the lily.

Jesus said that "the very hairs of your head are all numbered" (Luke 12:7). He said that the Father observed the sparrow's fall. The Bible teaches that God, the Father Almighty, was interested in the care of His prophet Elijah and sent an angel to bake him barley cake for him to eat. We read in the New Testament that when Peter was in jail, the great God sent down an angel with a cloak—Peter's cloak—and told him to put it around himself because it was cold outside. He also put his shoes on his feet before the angel led him through the locked doors, showing that God the Father, because He's omniscient, omnipresent, and eminent, can take care of all the details of all His people without any bother and without ever getting confused.

God being God can do everything as easily as He can do anything. He can do all things without effort. The eyes of God go throughout all the earth, and He sees not only everybody who lives, but also every hair on all the heads of all the people who live. He sees not only all the sparrows that were ever hatched, but He also sees all the feathers on their wings. If a feather is missing, He knows where it fell. The Bible teaches us that God is personally interested in us and in our details.

Now, returning to the seven provinces of prayer, let us focus on our spiritual lives. God is interested in your spiritual welfare, and He is ready to hear you pray about it. When David got himself into a jam because of his sin, he got on his knees and talked to God about it, just like you would talk to a doctor. He let God probe him, analyze him, diagnose him, and find out what was wrong with him so that God might make him well again. You and I can and should go to God in the same way.

Of course we should not waste all our time on ourselves. It is a decidedly selfish kind of praying that is always talking about me and my and I. But before we can pray rightly for anybody else, we have to be right ourselves, and therefore we can go to God with all the details of our spiritual lives. You have a perfect right to talk to Him about anything that is bothering you, and He will give you a sympathetic hearing and warm, friendly attention to all the details. Your personal spiritual life matters to Him.

Second, we can pray for our bodies. Many do not believe that God is interested in human bodies. Oh, but when God knelt down, as the poet said, out of the river, He scooped clay. There our great God, like a woman bending over her baby, worked the lump of clay until it became the shape of a man, and then He blew into it the breath of life. Man became a living soul, and God sanctified the human body. Similarly, when God the Son came into the body of the Virgin Mary, taking a body of His own that grew into manhood and became a fully mature human body with all the functions, He swept away forever any doubt that says God is not interested in our bodies.

There is a passage, 1 Corinthians 6:13, that says, "The body is . . . for the Lord, and the Lord for the body." The Lord is interested in the human body; do not imagine that He is not. He is interested in you. He is interested in your body, and you and I have a right to go to God believing that. God is also interested in your baby. God is interested in its temperature.

I believe that in the will of God, I have a right to expect deliverance if I am within His order, so that I might give Him praise. I don't believe that I can just eat as I please, live as I please, or do what I please—using my faculties and powers for my amusement and joy and pleasure, going through the world to see what I can get out of it—and then run to the Lord and expect Him to do a miracle of deliverance. I do not believe that, and I would not respect a God who would stoop to that kind of thing. But the child of God who walks in humility before Him can go to the heavenly Father and get whatever deliverance is needed.

The human body lies within the province of prayers God will answer.

Some do not pray for anything outside of their family. Certainly, God cares about our family and listens to our prayer in that regard. We are encouraged to pray for our family with the understanding that God does hear such prayers. Our prayers, however, should extend beyond our family and our personal needs.

Then there are material needs. Some people, when they've gotten themselves in a bit of trouble, want to rub Aladdin's lamp and make God their servant. The Lord is not your junior partner who runs errands for you. He will not make sure you get the help you need so that your prosperity will grow. Some think that in order to keep God on your side, you give Him a tithe of your money. In other words, God works on a ten percent commission. If He keeps you prosperous, He gets more, and the more He prospers you, the more He gets.

No, God does not need your money. The only reason you have a dime to give to God is because He gave you the dime in the first place. It's like getting a Christmas present from your four-year-old boy. Where did he get the money? You gave it to him. You give him the money for the Christmas present, and he comes to you just as innocently as if he had worked and earned it. When you give anything to God, God gave it to you in the first place. Therefore, God does not need your money.

The Lord has lots of money. Think of it all. Think of the uranium God has, the gold, the silver, and the pearls. If you think you can buy God off, get in good with the Lord, or receive special favors from God because of your generosity, you may just as well sew your wallet shut right now. God is not going to work on a percentage or a commission, but if you want things for His honor, He will bless your business, and He will help you, and He will work with you. He is interested in your soul, and He is interested in what His giving to you will do for you.

The workman has a perfect right to go to God. In fact, he should consecrate his business or his profession to the heavenly Father. He blesses the farmer who glorifies God in his living. He blesses the laboring man who glorifies God in his home and in his work. He blesses the businessman who glorifies God in his business. He blesses the professional man who takes God into his profession. But He does not run errands for anybody, and He is not a water boy for a proud Christian businessman. If we are humble and meek, and live for the glory of God, living to praise Him and for the good of our fellow men, God will work on our books and our sales. He will work on our jobs and help us.

Our friends also lie within the providence of prayer. I am referring to our interceding for others. Yet we must pray for other people without sticking our noses in their business. Some people are careless and do not care for anybody. Other people are so careful about everybody that they are in danger of intruding. Let us watch out for that. Do not intrude in other people's affairs. But if you know where prayer would be helpful, or if someone comes to you for prayer and counsel, then you have a perfect right to take that person on your heart as though you were that person, interceding in a unity that makes the two of you one.

God will answer prayers for your friends. You have a right to go to Him on behalf of your friends, your neighbors, your relatives, and intercede, providing that you carry the load as Jesus carried it.

We can also pray for our country. God will hear us when we pray for our nation. I will not bring politics into the pulpit, but I have a right to go to God about what I am seeing. I have a right to go to Him individually as a Christian, or as a church, and pray that He would throw His shielding arms around this land of the free. Our worst enemy is not Russia. Our worst enemy is ourselves. America needs to clean up, brighten up, pray up, and get right with God, and our preachers must preach the Word of God again. If we'd repent, all the armies of the world couldn't destroy us, for our beams would be laid deep in theology if our country was dedicated to the glory of God. No matter how many enemies gathered against us, they could not destroy America unless we destroyed ourselves from within. But if we are rotten from within, we will collapse and go down as the Romans did.

Our Father, we would ask Thee that a real spirit of prayer, that kind of intercessory prayer only Thou can give birth to, would take hold of every one of our hearts. Teach us the real value of prayer and make these Thy people a praying people. This we ask in Jesus' name. Amen.

FIFTEEN

Casting All Your Cares on Him

Therefore humble yourselves under the mighty hand of God, that He may exalt you in due time, casting all your care upon Him, for He cares for you.

1 Peter 5:6–7

A common error among Christians is that they apply promises to persons whom God did not have in mind. The Father's promises are for the Father's children, and we ought to always remember that. When the Jews in Jesus' day claimed certain promises for themselves because they were children of Abraham, Jesus said, "That's where you're mistaken. If you were children of Abraham, you would act like your father, Abraham. But you're not children of Abraham. All the promises made to Abraham did not apply to those who were the physical descendants of Abraham, but to those who were the seed of Abraham according to the Spirit." The promise in the verse above is for God's children.

Keep in mind, however, that these promises do not just apply to the prominent or successful children of God. Many good Christians are not successful or prominent. (Many wonderful people are not gifted at all. God has given His gifts as He sees fit, sovereignly through nature and grace.) We tend to push the gifted into prominent and successful positions, but I do not know that God does. What is emphasized in Scripture is faithfulness and love and the willingness to give all to Him. Apart from that, there's not much mention made of such success or prominence. So do not imagine this does not apply to you just because you aren't in a high position. The weak, the struggling, and the obscure are just as dear to God as the prominent and successful.

Returning to the promise itself, consider the presence of care in the world. Care in this context, of course, refers to anxieties and fears. We should keep in mind that fears and anxieties don't exist without reason. Optimism in every situation is irresponsible and unrealistic. Nobody can possibly be a sound judge of human affairs and be optimistic all the time. Similarly, all schemes to conquer fear while ignoring its cause are deceptive, and those who would follow them are living in a fool's paradise. The causes of our fears are real, and we have to admit their presence.

There is illness, for instance. Malaria alone takes hundreds of thousands of lives every year throughout the world, not to mention the millions taken by cancer and heart disease, etc. And accidents occur as well, even among good people. The world is full of sickness and pain, which makes people anxious and apprehensive. When some people get scared, they become hard and churlish, and they develop a shell over them like a turtle, hoping they can keep away the dangers and keep to themselves within that shell. Others drive themselves to what they call success, perhaps becoming rich, hoping they can buy their way through. But you can succeed and have plenty, and still these fears creep in. The reasons for them are here. You cannot buy off illness, and you cannot buy off accidents. And no one could ever be so successful that they would not fear war. Nobody could be so high up in the world that they could not become a victim of betrayal or bereavement.

On one level, pleasure-seeking is nothing but a reaction to fear: eat, drink, and be merry, for tomorrow we die. If I am going to die tomorrow, I better make good of things while I can, taking what I can from life. So some people go wild, not wanting to face their anxieties, which is why if you can think of a way to entertain people, encouraging them to play, you can be sure to make a lot of money.

Other people become nervous wrecks, developing mental disorders of all kinds because they are scared. Illnesses and accidents and the possibility of job loss, betrayal, separation, bereavement, death—is there anybody who can meet these enemies? Somebody has to. They will not go away on their own. "Ignore him, and he will go away" does not apply to death or even illness.

But God says, "Now walk before me, and I won't let one thing happen that isn't good for you. When you need it, I will let it happen, but I will watch over you as a physician over his patient. I will watch over you as a nurse over her child. You don't have to be an optimist and ignore things; you can be a realist and admit their presence. You don't have to collapse and be sent to an institution, for I'll handle the things you fear."

Yes, God is in control, and He cares about you and your needs. Cast all your care upon Him, for He cares for you. That is the sum of the Lord's word to us on that subject. That same theme runs through the Old Testament and the New Testament. The Savior taught it, and all the apostles teach it. It is simply this: God is personally concerned about you—you the individual, not just the masses.

We think in masses now, like when we see graphs or charts in the news in which a figure represents five million persons. But the Lord never thinks in blocks, in masses; He thinks in individuals. He thinks of His one sheep, of His one child. That is the teaching of the Scriptures. God is personally concerned about you. God is not too high and lofty to remember that His children are in a land where illness is prevalent and accidents happen every day. There are job losses and financial worries, and loved ones are separated or people are betrayed. A boy who had been close to us for many years grinned and shook our hand, then walked down the sidewalk to report to the military service.

Separations come; some people never return. God knows this and says, "I know that's the kind of world you live in, but I have laid hold of you forever. I know every detail of your trouble, all your problems, and I will anticipate every act of the enemy and every act of every enemy yet to come. I will go before you." Not only so, but He accepts our enemies as His enemies: "I will be an enemy to your enemies." That can only mean one thing: that if an enemy turns on me, God turns on him. If I am partly in the wrong, God will let that enemy through to me enough to chasten me, but He will never let him destroy me. He will never let a blow fall that I do not deserve.

God never strikes amiss, and He never lets anything happen to you that is not good for you. He says, "I am handling this. You take your hands off and stop worrying. You're on my side, and I'm on your side."

So cast all your care upon Him. This must be done by a firm act of the will. We do not grow into this. If you were walking along and you had a great burden, and I told you to let me carry that awhile, you would not shift it gradually onto me. You would either give it to me or keep it, and the act of transfer from you to me would be in an instant. One minute you had the burden, and the next minute I have it.

You have to do this by a firm act of your will. Why don't you do that now? You are trusting God but under a heavy load. Why not roll that burden onto the Lord? Don't you want to do that? You are walking with the Lord. You are a humble person trusting in His grace; you know you are His child, and His promises are for you. So why should we not roll our cares upon Him?

Lord, we are a company of Christian people. We have said yes to Thee and no to the world. Thou hast given us eternal life, and we are blessed, but we confess,

Father, that we are in a deadly, dangerous world; we're like tiny rabbits of the woods or like the deer in the forest. We live by staying alert. We exist only because we're watching. This works to make us nervous and anxious and fills us with apprehensions and fears, and it isn't pleasing that it should be so. Thou would look after us. Thou art around us, beneath us, before us, and behind us; help us, and we pray that we would cast all our cares upon Thee.

We roll upon Thee industrial fears and domestic fears; some are worried about their children, worrying about what they will do and where they will go when they are no longer under parental care. My God, Thou hast these thousands of years seen the generations grow up. Parents have dreamed over their growing children because they were soon to go out from under their care. My Lord, help us pray so we might roll our children's future onto Thee. Help us to roll on Thee the fear of disease and all other devilish things. Save us as we pray from all these fears. We would roll our cares upon Thee. You will take the whole miserable, backbreaking load of apprehensions and anxieties. Amen.

SIXTEEN

The Blessing That Lies in Prayer

Have mercy upon me, O God,
According to Your lovingkindness;
According to the multitude of Your tender mercies,
Blot out my transgressions.

Purge me with hyssop, and I shall be clean. . . .

And renew a steadfast spirit within me.

Restore to me the joy of Your salvation. . . .

Psalm 51:1, 7, 10, 12

There are two concepts of prayer that seem to be mutually exclusive of each other. One is what we call the objective concept, and the other, the subjective. When some people talk about prayer, they focus on the subjective: I, the subject, am praying, and I am focused on what prayer does to me. It soothes me, calms me, inspires me, and maybe illuminates me in some measure. Thus, it is subjectively valuable to me.

That is almost all you hear about prayer today. We talk about what prayer did to calm me. What prayer did to soothe me. What prayer did to relax me. The subjective element is the focus of most articles and sermons.

But then there is the objective element. This refers to what prayer does to change things. Those who believe in the objective power of prayer believe in its power to change the world around us.

Many people do not believe prayer has any objective meaning: It cannot make the sun stand still, and it cannot get anyone delivered from a disease. Others ignore what prayer does for the person who prays, talking only about being able to do any old thing through prayer. So which view should we adopt? Or more important, which does the Bible teach?

Thankfully, these two views are not mutually exclusive. One does not cancel the other out, and you are not forced to take one position and reject the other. Both of them are true. Prayer indeed has a subjective power over me. It is also true that prayer offered in the name of Jesus Christ can go out and change the face of the world. The Bible teaches that prayer has an amazing influence and power over the individual. It also teaches that prayer adequately made in the will of God can bring answers when it is the will of God that it should be so.

I will write more about these two effects of prayer, but first, lest you get a wrong notion, I would like to say something that may be disillusioning or even discouraging. I don't want to take away from you a crutch that you might have leaned on, but a good man will kick your crutch out from under you when you've outgrown your need for it. You may become a slave to the crutch, and you need to be delivered from that bondage.

The truth I'm referring to is that prayer in itself is nothing at all. Some claim prayer itself to be something: Prayer does this and prayer does that. Yet I want you to understand me—prayer in itself isn't anything at all. The glory of prayer lies in this: It engages God. The wonder of prayer is that it brings the human soul into contact with the everlasting Lord. But while prayer itself isn't anything, the one we pray to is everything.

If we are not in contact with God, if we have not engaged God, if our souls are not clean, and if we are not in His will, then prayer means nothing at all. You can pray until you are red-faced. You can pray all night. In fact, some people substitute prayer for obedience to God's will.

For instance, a man may have wronged somebody, he may have done some evil thing or said something unkind, unfriendly, or unpleasant. Yet instead of going back and confessing, apologizing, and getting it straightened out, he will attend prayer meetings. Instead of saying, "I'm sorry," he will be there if you announce a half night of prayer. He will be right there on his knees, but he will not obey God. Prayer may be substituted for obedience, and that kind of prayer means nothing whatsoever.

In fact, there may be times when prayer is offensive to God Almighty. Read the first chapter of Isaiah and see if it is not true.

Prayer is offensive to God when it is offered in disobedience. It is offensive to God Almighty when there is no intention to obey, when we are not clean and we do not intend to be clean. In our pollution, we may go to God and pray the Lord's Prayer and all the other prayers we know, read the Psalms of David, make up prayers of our own, and talk to God by the hour. Still, if we are not living as we should be, prayer can be a snare and a delusion. It means nothing at all to the soul.

All prayers that ascend to God, all the moaning and mumbling sent to God, unless they go up in purity and faith and obedience and righteousness, are wasted whimperings.

Returning to our subject, let's grant that the person praying has met these conditions. The blood of Jesus Christ has made him clean and he is in the will of God as far as he knows. He is a student of the Word and is open to seeing what God would have him do. The man's motive is right, and he is praying in the will of God. If this is the case, what does prayer mean for the individual?

Prayer is the greatest privilege ever granted to men. The Ancient of Days, high and lifted, stoops down and condescends to listen to the prayers of such worms as you and me. He listens to sinners by nature, and for a while by choice, little men and women with breath in our nostrils and tiny hearts beating.

Prayer lets us talk to the great God Almighty. The one who made the sun, rolled it around in His hand, and flung it against the darkness; who made the stars and studded the skies with them and cut out the rivers and pushed up the mountains and girded the world and made man upon it and gave him air to breathe and water to drink. That great God who holds the world in the hollow of His hand, bends His ear like a mother bending over a sick child, trying to catch the faintest whisper of the one she loves. That, I say, is the greatest privilege in all the world.

Therefore, prayer should be the most sacred thing in the world and should be made with the greatest sense of thanksgiving and gratitude. Not only is prayer the highest honor that can be granted to any being, but it is also the most profitable investment in all the world.

But there is also something to be gained personally through prayer. I've had the experience of having the whole world on my back. When that happens, you drop to your knees with your open Bible and read the Word and look up to God and get calm and oriented. You adjust to God in your soul, and pretty soon the world begins to roll off. By the grace of God, there is such a thing as making a profitable investment in prayer just for its subjective value, just for what it will do for you inside, just for the tuning up of your instrument, just for the harmonizing of your soul.

Prayer changes things, all right, and the greatest thing in the world is when it changes you on the inside. Yet while prayer is undoubtedly the greatest honor and the most profitable thing to do, it is also one of the hardest things in the world for Christians. (I do not doubt that much of the activity in religious circles today is a substitute for prayer.) The reason is because you have to be right with God to pray. It is hard because it means obedience.

Saying the words of the Lord's Prayer doesn't mean anything. Anybody can say it. Just memorize it and away you go. But getting your heart in gear, getting it right with God, and being in a position where the Lord's Prayer means anything to you—that's hard. It's so hard that people would rather do almost anything else. They would rather organize something, write something, say something, do something, paint something, dig something. God's people will do anything to keep from praying.

But even though it's hard, prayer has run the Church for two thousand years like nothing else. We like to pretend other things run the Church. We imagine money does. Based on what you hear from some preachers, you would think that money was indispensable. If money is all you've got, give it. The Church can use it for God's glory around the world. I do not say withhold it, but I do say this: If you don't have anything but money, you don't have much of anything. It is not money that runs the Church.

Brains don't run the church either. Neither do gifts and personality. Many believe these are the days when personality runs the Church, but it isn't so. We want personality, but personality never ran anything except a show. The Church of Jesus Christ does not run on personality. How carnal can we get and still claim to be followers of Jesus? There was no beauty in Him that we should desire Him, and He was so common-looking that Judas had to kiss Him so everybody would know who He was.

But the Church will still march along, driven by the winds of prayer, by the mighty gales of prayer from the hearts of men and women who are in touch with the Lord Jesus.

Prayer overlaps time and place. You can pray in an airplane, and you can pray in a submarine. You can pray on a hospital bed, in a schoolroom, or in a kitchen. You can pray anywhere. Prayer is the great leveler of men. The most illiterate person in the world can pray, and the most cultured person in the world cannot do better. No matter how smart or special you are, it will not make your prayers any dearer to God.

The most uncultured fellow in the world can pray just as well as the most learned, and there is no person alive—not the queen of England nor the president of the United States—who can do a greater act than pray an effective prayer.

A homeless person in Alabama gets his old battered Bible out and reads aloud and marks it with his fingers; he goes along painfully reading with only a year or two in school. Then he gets on his knees, looks up through the cracks of his poor shack, and talks to God. When he does this, he is doing greater deeds than a prayerless president can do. He is doing greater acts than a prayerless prime minister.

Prayer is the great leveler. In the presence of prayer, there are no popes and bishops and pastors and doctors. In the presence of God, there are no little men. In the presence of God, there are no big men. In the presence of God, there are only redeemed men and women.

Prayer is not only the greatest force in the universe, but that force is available to all the children of God. Prayer makes old people young, and young people wise beyond their years. I would rather trust the wisdom of a praying man twenty-five years old than I would the wisdom of a man seventy-five years old who did not pray, for I do not think we ought to listen to any man who does not first listen to God. The praying young man will have greater wisdom than the prayerless old man, but the praying old man will have that happy youthfulness of a young man. A praying old man is a young man inside, and the praying young man gets old in experience and knowledge.

Prayer robs adversity of its power and makes a poor man rich. Prayer will gear you up, so that dying will be nothing more than passing out of God's left hand into His right hand. In prayer, you will cross the river from one side to the other.

Prayer keeps the dead saints alive. The praying saint does not die but lives on in his prayers. The power of God comes to this place and that place long after a man is gone.

Last, prayer gives you heaven.

In the heart of Africa, David Livingstone was found kneeling in prayer. Oh, what a dramatic and beautiful land for an equally beautiful life. He gave his life for Africa as a medical doctor. The African people, with great wisdom, tenderly laid out the old, tired body with all the gentleness of a mother, then took out his great, silent heart. They literally cut it out of Livingstone's bosom and sewed him up.

They buried this part under a babul tree, and then they carried his body through hostile tribes to the shores of Africa, shipping him to Westminster Abbey, where everything lies but his heart. Wasn't there poetic justice in that? Wasn't there beautiful wisdom that they buried his heart there? The heart of Livingstone still prays even while the spirit of Livingstone is with his Savior.

O Father, I pray earnestly that I might position myself in such a way that I can connect to You in prayer. Remind me of my sin, and allow me to confess it and make my heart right. Let me come into Thy presence as a person washed by the blood of the Lord Jesus Christ. May my prayer be the most significant thing about my life today. Amen.

SEVENTEEN

God Working through Us

For it is God who works in you both to will and to do for His good pleasure.

Philippians 2:13

f we are going to experience a fruitful prayer life, we need to understand how God works in and through our prayer. Once we understand this, it will dramatically change our prayer life. So often Christians pray contrary to God's way, and because of that, their prayers are not answered. To enjoy a fruitful prayer life, then, we must come to understand how God works and how He doesn't work.

Perhaps the first basic thing is to deal with the fact that God does not answer my prayer according to my expectation. He does not allow me to use my prayer life to accomplish my goals. Unfortunately, that's too often the expectation of many Christians.

The focus of God is not to make us happy; rather, He does everything for His glory. His work is always creative and constructive according to His character and nature. That He can use us to accomplish those goals is the key to understanding the dynamics associated with our prayer life.

Perhaps the hardest thing for us as Christians is to separate ourselves from the human element of prayer. Yet God is not constrained by our limitations. Christ did not die on the cross to save us just so we can go about our own business.

It seems the attitude of many Christians today, once they are saved, is to say in effect, "I can take it from here. My salvation gets me into heaven," and that's about the end of it. Some do not know that salvation is the beginning stage of God using us to accomplish His purposes. If we can handle it, then we don't need the Holy Spirit. If we can handle it, then what we're doing has nothing to do with God.

Our prayer line is the channel through which God works in this world. The works that He does through our prayer life are what glorify Him in the utmost. This has been challenged from the beginning. Lucifer said, "I will ascend above the heights of the clouds, I will be like the Most High" (Isaiah 14:14). Everything was to glorify himself. This has infected humanity to its utter destruction.

We pound our chests, and everything we do is focused upon us and who we are. This seems to be the theme of a lot of Christians' prayers today. We are working through ourselves to accomplish our goals.

It is a transforming experience when we realize that God wants to work through us to accomplish His work and goals, particularly through our prayers. God does not do anything apart from His people. Certainly, we have the storms and hurricanes and fire and all of that. But when God wants to accomplish His purpose and goal, He always does it through His people.

In the Old Testament, God accomplished His purpose for Israel through the man Moses. When God called Moses to do this, Moses said, "O my Lord, I am not eloquent, neither before nor since You have spoken to Your servant; but I am slow of speech and slow of tongue" (Exodus 4:10). Moses did not have what he thought he needed to do what God was calling him to do.

It took Moses forty years in the wilderness to get all of Egypt out of him. Perhaps nobody was more educated than Moses at the time. Moses did not understand that God was not interested in his education, abilities, or skills. God was interested in Moses as an obedient servant through whom He could accomplish His purposes.

That is the problem with Christians today. They think God is interested in their education and skills in that the more they have of these, the more God can use them. However, God cannot accomplish His goals through our abilities alone. He can only accomplish His purposes through us when we yield ourselves completely to Him. It is only when I as a Christian surrender everything to God, and hold on to nothing bad, that He can accomplish His work through me.

Think of David in the Old Testament. When God called him to go up against Goliath, it wasn't because David was well armed and prepared militarily to face Goliath. David did not have anything in any way to compete with that old rugged Philistine Goliath.

God sent David against Goliath to show that He uses people regardless of the equipment they have. David's victory over Goliath wasn't David's victory; it was God's victory, without question. God's strength is not in our weapons.

Look at the weapons David had compared to the weapons Goliath had. David's slingshot was no comparison to Goliath's armor, yet God used David's slingshot to defeat the most sophisticated armor at the time. David was not able to defeat Goliath because of who David was, but rather because of God, who used David to defeat Goliath.

The apostle Paul says in 1 Corinthians 12:4–6 that God works in people and through people. God has work to do and does it in and through His people by the gifts of the Spirit. So the same Lord, though there are differences of administrations; the same God, though there are diversities of operation; the same gifts, though there are diversities of gifts, for it is the same Spirit.

I don't know of any church board that would have approved of someone like David going up against a man like Goliath. They would've compared what David had to what Goliath had, and they would not have allowed that little boy to face the Philistine giant.

That's what religion does. It compares one with the other. It tries to develop the weapons that are needed to defeat the enemy. This is precisely why the enemy is not being defeated in our generation. We are trying to defeat the enemy on his grounds so we can take the credit for it.

Another mistake many Christians make is to believe God wants to use their past to get a present victory. God does not give us a reservoir of wisdom and power. If He did, it would soon be stagnant. God does not come to a man and pipe him full of wisdom and then say, "If you get in any trouble, come see me or call me up and pray, but in the meantime, you have the whole cistern full of power. You draw on that wisdom because it's yours." God never did it that way. Instead, God gives a man a word of wisdom and gives to him power, but God is the power in that man. He is the word of wisdom in that man. It is God working in the man, not the man working. God becomes wisdom to us and becomes power to us.

That is why Christians blunder so pitifully. A baseball player plays twelve years in the league, and we say, "He's skillful, he has learned, he knows." The same goes with anything else. People learn by experience; we learn how to do things by doing them. But in the kingdom of God, it is completely different. A man can be seventy-five years old, having served God most of his life, yet he makes pitiful blunders and remains ignorant and untaught. If God is not working through the man and in the man, the man himself is right back to where he was when he started. It is God who works in you.

When it comes to prayer, we most often misunderstand the whole purpose of it. We have the idea that prayer is to talk

God into giving us what we need at the time. We believe this is just a way to access what we need and want to do in our lives. It has never occurred to many Christians that prayer is not on our terms; prayer is God's weapon to reach out into the world around us. God uses us and our prayer life to touch the world for His kingdom.

Because this is true, God does not rest upon our abilities or knowledge or wisdom or strength. None of these things affect how God wants to work through us.

Gideon, for example, when God called him to be used by God, did not believe he was qualified. As he looked at himself, he did not see the credentials he thought he needed to do the work God was calling him to do. But with Gideon and others like him, God never calls the qualified; He qualifies the called.

Our qualifications do not matter to God. What does matter is to yield ourselves completely to Him for His pleasure and His work.

It took quite a while to reach the point where Gideon could trust God regardless of how unqualified he felt. And that's exactly how God works. He delights in using those who have no qualifications and no weapons for the project before them. Because when God can find someone with no qualifications, that is the person He can use to bring glory to himself.

If we were to strip from churches all that man is doing and leave only what God has done and is doing, I'm afraid we would trim the average church down to a minimum. There probably would not be enough left to hold a decent service. It seems that most churches today are running on their own steam, which they have learned by going to school and seminary and reading books that give ten easy lessons on growing your church.

The Church of God is going to bless, and the Christians whom God is going to bless will be those who have come to the end of their hoarded resources. Then they will experience the grace of God in their lives and ministries. God can only begin to work when we have come to the end of our resources and have nothing to fall back on.

People cannot build the Church. It takes the Holy Spirit to work in a man who has surrendered everything and allowed God to do the work through the ministry of prayer. God is not building His Church simply to have a religious organization.

If my prayers are potent, I must pray in such a way that God is working through that prayer. My prayer cannot be based upon my wisdom or understanding, but upon God's wisdom. Sometimes my prayers will sound ridiculous because they are not from a human perspective. Let us allow God to use us for His glory through our prayer.

O Lord, how mighty and wonderful Thou art. I cannot comprehend all that Thou art in all that Thou wouldst do through me. But I surrender my prayer life to be used by You as You see fit. Amen.

EIGHTEEN

God's Wisdom Working through Us

For it is God who works in you both to will and to do for His good pleasure.

Philippians 2:13

Our prayer is a channel through which God accomplishes His work in His way. He is not accomplishing *our* work, like so many people might think. And He is not doing things according to the wisdom of men.

All that God does, He does in His own wisdom and knowledge of the future. Nothing is done by chance or without knowing how it will turn out. Write that down: Everything God does, He does in His "foreseeing wisdom." God knows our tomorrows and the days after that, all down through the years. All has been planned before time existed.

Long before the universe existed, God had planned what He is doing now. God does not get mixed up. He has a well-designed plan that nothing can hinder, and His wisdom is above man's every step of the way. There has never been a time when God was confused and had to consult anyone. Everything He does is a fulfillment of His wisdom from the very beginning.

All around the world, people play things by ear—trying things out and seeing how they go. Mankind's wisdom is limited, but God's is not. Long before there was matter, motion, or law, God had foreseen it all. The Bible teaches us that nothing happens that God did not foresee.

No, the world is not a truck racing downhill with the driver having a heart attack at the wheel. The world is moving toward a predetermined end, and God Almighty stands in the shadows. He is watching it and guiding it—the nation of Israel and the rest of the nations of the world, and the great worldly church we call Christendom, and the true Church that He hides in His own heart. God knows where they are at all times by His infinite and perfect wisdom. He is running everything according to His plans, which He made before Adam ever stood upon the earth. Before Abraham or David or Isaiah or Paul, before Jesus was born in Bethlehem's manger, God had it all planned out.

I do not want you to think of God sitting down with a pencil and working it out the way you and I would have to. God thinks, and it is done. He wills, and it comes to pass. God does not have to work with a pencil and a compass the way architects and builders do. He is not like a man as he begins a project. A contractor, for example, starts a project by researching and then thinks he has everything in line. But as he works on the project, he discovers something new and must go in a different direction.

This is not how it is with God. Things are always done according to His plans because He thinks and He speaks them into existence. "In the beginning was the Word, and the Word was with God, and the Word was God. . . . All things were made through Him, and without Him nothing was made that was made" (John 1:1, 3). He is the Word, and He speaks things into being.

As a Christian, when something bad happens, it can lead you to wonder why God let it happen. How could He? There must have been a huge mistake somewhere. But that is a lack of trust and obedience. Sometimes God allows bad things to happen to mold us and shape us, or because we've rebelled against Him, getting us into all kinds of trouble. We may bring on ourselves happenings that are temporarily not in His will. But even then, if the root of the matter is in us, God absorbs this and turns it into victory.

If I am to have potency in my prayer life, I need to understand that everything needs to be in complete harmony with the wisdom of God. I do not pray according to my own wisdom and understanding, or most of my prayer would be ineffective.

I believe this lack of looking to God's wisdom is a reason why there is so much prayer and so few answers to prayer. We look at situations from our viewpoint and our wisdom and then base our prayers on our own conclusions. We may be praying in the wrong direction.

We must pray with God's intended outcome in mind. This outcome is not something that can be guessed at, nor can we have a conference and vote on it. The only way I can understand the overall intention of God's will is to spend time in His Word.

To understand God's overall will is the biggest factor in energizing my prayer ministry. Once I get to know God's will, I can begin to pray in that direction. When I pray in that direction, I have the power of God flowing through me, accomplishing what He wants to accomplish.

I am saddened sometimes to hear prayer requests that are far from the will of God. We can't expect God to stop what He is doing and jump to our requests. Spending time in the Word is the key to preventing this.

But just reading the Bible doesn't solve the issue unless we're reading it in the right spirit. Often we come to the Bible in order to get something we want, such as a verse that will help us be positive about the day, e.g., "I can do all things through Christ who strengthens me" (Philippians 4:13). But we may not know what the verse is really about. We begin to pull it out of context to make it say what we want it to say in order to satisfy our ambitions. Certainly, God is not interested in that attitude or that kind of praying.

It takes a long time to know how to pray for certain things. I need to look closely at a situation or person to discern God's will. Maybe God does not want to change our circumstances but instead wants to give grace to go through a trial victoriously. King Solomon put this in the right perspective when he wrote, "That which has been is what will be, that which is done is what will be done, and there is nothing new under the sun" (Ecclesiastes 1:9).

Through prayer, God is doing that which He planned to do from the very beginning. There is no change in the wind. Nothing has happened that has disturbed and canceled the will of God. From the very beginning of all things, He had complete wisdom and knowledge guiding Him.

Even the fall of man in the garden of Eden in no way changed God's plan for the world. And nothing that has happened down through the years has made Him rethink His plans.

Nothing in this world, not even the devil himself, can change God's plan. His plan was established in eternity, and nothing on earth or in time can alter it.

I am so grateful that neither God nor His plans ever change. When I begin to understand that, I have confidence in following God because I know He knows what He is doing.

Heavenly Father, what a joy it is to understand that Your wisdom is absolutely perfect in every degree. Thank You so much, and thank You for revealing to me Your plan step by step. I'm trusting You for the faith to believe even though I do not understand what Your plan is. Amen.

NINETEEN

God Working through Us Is Not an Accident

Jesus Christ is the same yesterday, today, and forever.

Hebrews 13:8

Sometimes the things God does in the world look like an accident or a mistake, but that is due to our blindness and our ignorance. We do not know why God does what He does, so we begin to fidget and wonder if God is really paying attention. God sees tomorrow, but we see only today. God sees every side, but we see only one side. God knows what we do not know, and God has all the pieces of the puzzle. You and I have only a few pieces.

We like to see our lives bloom into a beautiful picture with everything in place, but often the pieces are scattered around. Nothing seems to fit together. Sometimes when you're putting a puzzle together, two pieces look as if they fit together, but they do not, yet you try to force them together anyway and break an edge off. That leaves you worse off than you were before. Similarly, we sometimes take the work of God and try to make it into something it wasn't meant to be.

I spent a good part of my life doing just that. I forgot that it's God who gives us wisdom. It's God who works in us, if we let Him. That is why I believe in the gifts of the Spirit.

I have always had the belief that all the gifts of the Spirit ought to be in the Church today just as they were at Pentecost. Some people will tell you that the gifts of the Spirit ended years ago, but they are wrong. Such people quote 1 Corinthians 13:13: "And now abide faith, hope, love, these three; but the greatest of these is love," saying that all these things will be put away, knowledge will vanish, and everything will cease. They argue that *all these things ceased* refers to certain gifts. Don't they know that they ceased by fulfillment? They did not stop being, so we cannot get rid of faith, hope, and love, and we dare not say that the gifts of the Spirit are no more.

God is working through His people, and what God works will last. What God doesn't work won't last. I do not care how great a man is, he cannot do immortal work because he is a mortal man. He cannot think immortal thoughts because he has a mortal mind. But if the Holy Ghost works in him and through him, distributing to every man gifts as He will, then God will do His work. We will be able to do the things of God and think the thoughts of God.

There are no accidents in the Christian life. If a man follows the Lord, God works his life out for him. To God, all things have already happened. If you knew you had to die tomorrow, you might feel a little low for a while, but then you would become elated because your future is set in Christ.

God's emotions never fluctuate, because everything has already happened with God. He does not go around watching dials and looking at gauges, checking if everything's all right, and testing to see if we are on the beat. God does not have to do that because His purposes never change. He is moving toward a predetermined end, which He purposed in Christ Jesus before the world began. I've said it before and I'll say it again: There are no accidents in God's plan.

When the angels sang over Bethlehem's manger, they were not announcing anything new. The news of Christ's coming had been known in the heart of God before there was even an Eden or an Adam or an Eve.

When God told Jonah to go to Nineveh and preach, Jonah bought a one-way ticket on a boat going in another direction.

But God never changes His mind, and never shall. Jonah, as you know, ended up preaching in Nineveh anyway. Israel sinned against God, and God punished them and disciplined them, and they ended up right where God said they would be.

There are differences of opinion on prophecy, but I will tell you what I believe based on the Holy Book in my hand. I believe that the seed of Abraham shall yet walk upon the mountains of Israel. I believe that God shall yet have His people back there. He has not changed His mind, and never shall.

When Jesus was sent to that cross to save the world, if He had gotten discouraged when He saw how He was received, He would not have been God. Jesus knew what He was walking into when He walked quietly to the cross and died.

History teaches that God works providentially through men. History marks the footprints of God, and the footprints of God are history. The way God worked through Abel, Noah, Abraham, Lot, and all the rest down the years, that's the way God works; He has not changed His mind.

God never lifts His hands off His work, and when He says, "Do this," He means go do it now. "I will work through you, and I'll not be discouraged. You may be discouraged, but I won't." He leads all things toward a preordained end.

If the devil were as smart as he thinks he is, he would not allow us to catch on to his plans. There is an old saying: The higher up the ape goes, the more his tail shows. When the devil rises up against you, you will see his tail hanging, you will notice him. And that's what happens when the devil hits God's people—they brace themselves, and the devil's plans are revealed. If you attack God's people enough, you will bring out everything good that is in them.

When everything is going all right with me, I am one of the laziest, most easygoing persons you ever saw in your life. But when things go against me, I back up a few steps and then go on the offensive. In other words, the very intention of the devil to drive me back has precisely the opposite effect.

I believe the same is true with Christians everywhere. God doesn't take His hands off His work—He's moving toward a preordained plan. And if we work with Him in that plan, Satan's efforts to stop us will only cause us to snap our teeth shut and say, in the name of God and in the strength of Jehovah, "We're moving forward." God's work will prevail as it heads toward a preordained end by the same wisdom, power, and love by which He created everything in the first place.

///////////////////

You are no accident; do not think you are. God made all things with a preordained purpose and by His foreknowing wisdom. God does what He does by wisdom and power and love, and there is no less wisdom, no less power, no less love now than there ever was.

This is hard for us to understand because we cannot see it. We must believe, and believing is a kind of seeing, but of course it's not the same as physically seeing something. I heard a man preach a sermon years ago, who said the Christian has three men inside of him: the old man, the new man, and the human. The old man is what he is until he is converted; then he becomes the new man in Christ. But all along, there is the human. The human is your genes and personality and what makes you, you. We never lose that part of us, and it can get us in trouble. Long after you have gotten the victory over the old man, the human can still mess with you. That is the part that gets carnally happy about things and also carnally gloomy.

The old man has to die in order to live in the power of the new man, and the new man keeps the human somewhat under control.

It's the human in us that has trouble believing sometimes. The human needs to physically see things, and so we have to push past the human in order to see by faith.

When my prayer is in order and in alignment with God's will and purpose, my next task is to be persistent. Whatever happens is no accident from God's point of view. And if something seems off, I need to reevaluate my prayer to make sure there is nothing in my life that is keeping my prayers from being used of God.

And along the way we must keep in mind that sometimes an accident from our point of view is simply God doing His will beyond our understanding.

I love Thee, O God, because of the faithfulness of Thy will. As I struggle to understand that, I will make mistakes. I am so glad that You do not depend upon my perfection but rather on Your perfection, and bring me in line with that. Praise Your precious name. Amen.

TWENTY

Is Anything Too Hard for the Lord?

Is anything too hard for the LORD? At the appointed time I will return to you, according to the time of life, and Sarah shall have a son.

Genesis 18:14

When we pray, sometimes God seems so far away. There is often a sense of remoteness from Him in the Christian's life.

In the verse above, God asked this question as both a rebuke and a promise, and His deeds proved His words were true. We must be honest and admit that a lot of religious talk is fanciful and unrelated to reality. But the power of the Christian message emerges in practical deeds, and that leads to faith and obedience.

I have examined this closely, so I am not uttering mere shreds of opinion. The word *hard* in the original Hebrew was different from our word *hard*, such as when we say, for instance, that it's hard to lift something. The Hebrew word can be translated "hard" or "difficult," and while they are similar, they are not quite the same. Hard means tough and severe, such as when Scripture says, "Pharaoh made their lives bitter with hard bondage." The hard bondage was the bondage of slavery; *hard labor* are the words we would use today. It didn't mean the Hebrews necessarily did skillful work, but they were made to do work requiring the sort of physical labor that tired one's bones and muscles. The other definition of the word *hard* means great, difficult, and wonderful, and that's the word used in the verse at the beginning of this chapter. Is anything too great for God? Is anything too difficult for God? Is anything too wonderful for God to do?

Of course, nothing is hard for God by either definition. God, having all the energy in the universe, can naturally do the hardest thing there is to do, and God, having all the wisdom there is, naturally has all the skills He needs to do anything.

Some things are hard for people because they require physical or mental energy that we just do not have. Other things require knowledge beyond our store. But it is impossible to conceive of anything that requires knowledge that God does not have when He knows all there is to know instantly and effortlessly.

Still, other things may require wisdom beyond us, for you see, there is a difference between knowledge and wisdom. Man may be very wise and not very knowledgeable, or he may be knowledgeable and not very wise. Wisdom is the ability to make sound judgments, and God possesses infinite wisdom.

But beyond our lack of energy, strength, knowledge, or wisdom, something may be too hard for us because of enemies standing in the way. Imagine a football game, for instance. It isn't difficult to carry the ball down a field if no opponents are there. One fellow wants to get the pigskin across the goal line, but two or three or ten other fellows block him. The devil is a great player, blocking us constantly, only it's not a game with him. He is dead serious. He hinders you. And he pits himself against you and often brings you down so you cannot complete your task. But is it conceivable that the great God Almighty, who created the stars and calls them by name and knows their number, can be stopped?

God does as He pleases with the armies of heaven and the armies of earth, and there is nobody who can stand in His way. He has His way in the world. He is the sovereign God, and all the demons in hell can deploy themselves in whatever formation they choose, like players on the football field, and God Almighty can walk triumphantly through toward His goal, because He is God. Jesus Christ walked straight to the cross without hindrance, rose from the dead without hindrance, and went to the right hand of God without hindrance, though many were trying to hinder Him every step of the way.

Why do we see so little of God's ability to do hard and difficult things? Because we are accustomed to living in our leprosy. We have closed minds; even though we are orthodox, we are unbelievers.

There are two kinds of unbelief. There is the bold, arrogant unbelief of the sinner, who comes out and says, "I don't believe your Bible. I don't believe your God. If there is a God, why is there disease, war, and all the rest? I do not want any more of your religion. I do not believe it." That is the man Jesus described in the book of Revelation as having a cold heart. He does not believe in Christianity at all and says so outright.

But then there is the unbelief of the religious man. He would not say, "I don't believe the Bible." He does believe the Bible. He buys them, gives them as presents, and reads them sedulously. He does not say, "I don't believe in your God." He does believe in God. But he just cannot believe Him for anything new.

He cannot believe that this is the hour, this is the day. God, to him, is always historic, and the Bible is a historic book. He cannot bring himself to believe in the God of the present, the living God, the God of today and tomorrow. He is perfectly willing to believe in the God of yesterday. Believing in the God of yesterday makes us orthodox. Believing in the God of today releases God's power into our midst.

We often bring to God a closed mind. We have developed a chronic case of non-expectation. We have a psychology of continuing defeat.

We do not expect anything new from God, and so we begin to come to terms with our defeat and our captors. We begin to learn to live in Babylon, including our churches, slowly learning the language of the Babylonians. We still use blessed gorgeous old Hebrew at home, but out in the marketplaces we use the language of Babylon. Because we do not have God Almighty's power released, we must think our way through the world on our own. We act as if Christ were still dead instead of His having risen from the dead.

Do you know what I think? I think we ought to magnify the resurrected Christ more than we do.

Why do the children of the King go around mourning all day? Because they think the King's Son is still in the grave. He is not in the grave, for He has long ago risen from the dead, and all power is given unto Him in heaven and in earth, and that power is waiting for you and me to dare to put away our psychology of non-expectation. Put away the attitude of being satisfied with defeat. What is the result of Christ still being dead? What is the result of this psychology of defeat? It is that the devil is satisfied, and the Spirit is grieved.

Did you notice that when Jesus charged Israel with unbelief, their wrath burned against Him, and they took Jesus out to throw Him over a cliff and kill Him? They said, "We're orthodox! What do you mean?" Believing to them meant accepting a creed and not expecting something from the God of the creed. They could go halfway, but they could not go the rest, and it was this charge of unbelief that caused them to snarl and grind their teeth at Jesus.

And that was the animosity that grew in intensity until they killed Him at last on a cross. But God, who finds nothing hard, raised Him easily from the dead on the third day.

The Spirit is grieved because of our unbelief. We look to each other for help instead of to God, and our altar fires burn low. We are forced to look to the flesh and misplace our confidence. Israel was always running to Egypt for help, sending messages to a heathen king, asking him to come over and help. They were always defeated when they did that.

We often focus on church strategies and methods rather than on God's power, acting as if Jesus Christ were dead. If Christ has not risen, why bother with the whole business of church at all? If Christ has not risen, why try to keep it going? If Christ has not risen, we are of all men most miserable. Let us eat, drink, be merry, and have as good a time as possible before we die.

But Christ has risen from the dead and become the first fruits of those who slept. He has risen, and therefore we do not need these other things. Our confidence is misplaced.

Methodology without the Holy Ghost is empty. Where there is faith, there is God. We ought to take this seriously and repent, my brethren. We ought to call a moratorium on prayer requests and repent instead, for the Spirit is waiting and hovering over our chaos, ready to say, "Let there be light," when we believe. Let us repent of our thinking, which accepts things as they are, forgetting that God says to not talk about the old things, for "I will do a new thing. . . . I give waters in the wilderness and rivers in the desert, to give drink to My people" (Isaiah 43:19, 21).

That is our God. That is the God we worship. That is the Christ we worship. Let us repent. Let us go to God and ask Him to forgive us. Israel got angry when Jesus talked like this to them. Are you going to do the same, or are you going to humble yourself and ask God to give you a refreshed mind?

We have this psychology of non-expectation and chronic defeatism despite the fact that Christ is at the right hand of God, looking down eagerly and ready to help us, the power of the Holy Ghost right here in our midst. Why can't we believe? Let us repent, and let us ask God to blow away the fog that shrouds us, take the dust off our souls, and help us dare to believe again. Then, after we believe and the grace of God is flowing, we can go back to thinking about strategies and methods. That is normal and right. Paul had his methods, but he did not try to substitute methods for the Holy Ghost. Let us not do that either, but instead let us look to Jesus Christ, risen and glorified, and expect Him to do the impossible.

O God, our Father, Thou knowest we are followers of Thy Son. We are not backing out, and we are not allowing the devil to tell us who we are. We are known of Your Son because we know Him. And we bless Thee.

But Thou knowest, Father, our chronic non-expectation. Dear Lord, we are as Israel was; we do not expect anything from Thee. We pray, pray, pray the same words week after week and expect nothing. Forgive us, Lord.

Thou knowest, Father, how easy it is to get into a mental rut, to let yesterday dictate tomorrow. But Thou has said that Thou art a God who maketh all things new, so we pray that Thou will touch our hearts and give us a faith that will rise and dare to begin to believe Thee to do the unexpected and even the impossible. Thou art the God of the impossible. O God, break out even now over the next days upon us, in such fullness that Satan will know he's not running things. Bear Thy mighty arms, O God, and give us faith. We trust Thee that we may not grieve Thee by our unbelief.

And now may the grace and mercy and peace of the Triune God, Father, Son, and Holy Ghost be with us forever. Amen.

TWENTY-ONE

A Man of Prayer

During a business session at a Christian Missionary Alliance general council meeting, the delegates were bogged down in motions and amendments, and amendments to the amendments. Tozer became increasingly impatient with the tedium of it all. Finally, his restless spirit could take no more. He turned to Raymond McAfee, sitting beside him.

"Come on, McAfee," he whispered, "let's go up to my room and pray before I lose all my religion."

Whatever acclaim he earned as an eloquent preacher and an outstanding writer can accurately be attributed to his close relationship with God. Tozer preferred God's presence to any other. The foundation of his Christian life was prayer. He not only preached prayer, but he also practiced it. He always carried with him a small notebook in which he jotted requests for himself and others, usually of a spiritual nature.

Tozer's prayers bore the same marks as his preaching: honesty, frankness, humor, intensity. His praying deeply affected his preaching, for his preaching was but a declaration of what he discovered in prayer. His praying also affected his living. He often said, "As a man prays, so is he." Everything he did flowed from his prayer life.

The bulk of his time each day was spent wrestling with God in prayer. Tozer literally practiced the presence of God. Often he would withdraw from family and friends to spend time alone with God. It was not unusual for him to lose all track of time in those meetings with God.

McAfee regularly met in Tozer's study each Tuesday, Thursday, and Saturday morning for a half hour of prayer. Often when McAfee entered, Tozer would read aloud something he recently had been reading—it might be from the Bible, a hymnal, a devotional, or a book of poetry. Then he would kneel by his chair and begin to pray. At times he prayed with his face lifted upward. Other times he prayed totally prostrate on the floor, a piece of paper under his face to keep him from breathing carpet dust.

God's Presence

McAfee recalls one especially memorable day. "Tozer knelt by his chair, took off his glasses, and set them on the chair. Resting on his bent ankles, he clasped his hands together, raised his face with his eyes closed, and began: 'O God, we are before Thee . . .' With that there came a rush of God's presence that filled the room. We both worshiped in silent ecstasy and wonder and adoration. I've never forgotten that moment, and I don't want to forget it."

On those occasions when McAfee was praying, he would hear Tozer rustling about. Opening an eye to see what was going on, he would discover Tozer, pencil in hand, writing. While McAfee prayed, Tozer had a thought he wanted to capture.

Tozer met with his church staff regularly for prayer. Once, during a staff prayer meeting, with Tozer prone on the floor in deep conversation with God, the telephone rang. Tozer broke off his prayer to answer the phone. He carried on a twenty-minute conversation with a pastor, giving him all sorts of instructions and advice that he himself never followed—taking time off, going on a vacation, and so on. The staff just sat there listening and chuckling to themselves, because Tozer never took a vacation in his life.

Hanging up the telephone, Tozer resumed his position on the floor and picked up where he left off by saying, "Now, God, as I was saying . . ."

Another time, Dr. Louis L. King, Tozer, and two other preachers were engaged in a half day of prayer. One of the preachers was known for his bombastic, colorful speech, both in his preaching and his praying. This man began praying for a certain world leader who at the time was hindering missionary work. "If you can't change him," the preacher prayed, "then kill him and take him to heaven!" Later, Tozer took King aside. "Did you hear what he prayed this morning?" he asked, a hurt expression on his face. "'Take him to heaven'? Why, he doesn't even believe in Jesus Christ. That wasn't prayer. He was saying that for our benefit. You never speak to God in that fashion. When you approach God, you should always use reverent language. It's God, not man, we're talking to in prayer!"

A Sacred Occupation

Prayer, according to Tozer, was the most sacred occupation a person could engage in. Often when Tozer prayed, people felt as though God was right at his elbow. Sometimes they were tempted to open their eyes to see.

Tozer's praying embraced the minutiae as well as the transcendental. One time, while King was visiting, Tozer had to go downtown to buy some special light bulbs for the church. Before the two men left the office, Tozer had them both kneel. In the simplest terms, he prayed, "Now, Lord, we don't know anything about light bulbs." And on he went, in a very human way, asking God for wisdom in such a mundane matter as the purchase of light bulbs.

Summer Bible camps and conferences were a special delight for Tozer. Every year he spent considerable time ministering at these places. To him, the whole atmosphere was conducive to prayer and getting closer to God.

He usually would walk out each morning to the surrounding woods to find a place to pray. Kneeling beside a fallen log, he would spend time in worship and prayer. Occasionally another person would join him in these rustic prayer meetings, and as they began, Tozer would often have some word to say about coming into the presence of God, which to him was always very real and immediate. Then he would invariably say, "Well, what shall we pray about?" Then followed a brief time of talking about subjects of prayer.

Usually Tozer prayed first.

One morning, the rain changed his plans, so he and Robert W. Battles, a close friend who was sharing the conference platform with Tozer, met in Tozer's cabin for prayer at nine o'clock. Each knelt on opposite sides of a cot.

"Well, Junior," Tozer began, "what should we pray for today?"

"I think we should pray for these people who have come to hear the likes of us preach."

The two men talked about prayer and what and whom they should be praying for. Then Tozer began to talk about God, the Incarnation, the glory and majesty of the Trinity, holiness, heaven, angels, immortality, the Church, and its mission in the world. No agenda, no sense of time, only the marvelous sense of the presence of God.

Then, before they got around to actually praying, the lunch bell rang.

"Oh no!" Battles complained. "We didn't even get down to praying and the bell has rung for lunch!"

"Well, Junior. We met to pray. Do you know something? What we have been doing all morning has been perilously close to praying."

There were times, as the two men tramped through the woods for a quiet walk together, that Tozer would get a far-off look in his eye, his nostrils would flare, and he would say in all solemnity, "Junior, I want to love God more than anyone in my generation."

At least once, Tozer lost all track of time as he was in his cabin praying. The time came for him to speak, and he was nowhere to be found. Another person had to substitute for him. When Tozer finally did show up, he would say only that he'd had a more important appointment.

Focus on God

When in prayer, Tozer would shut out everything and everyone and focus on God. His mystic mentors taught him that. They showed him how to practice daily the presence of God. He learned the lesson well.

Prayer for Tozer was inextricably tied to worship. "Worship," said Tozer in an uncharacteristically long sentence, "is to feel in your heart and express in some appropriate manner a humbling but delightful sense of admiring awe and astonished wonder and overpowering love in the presence of that most ancient Mystery, that majesty which philosophers call the First Cause, but which we call our Father in heaven."

Worship was the impetus behind all he was and did. It controlled every aspect of his life and ministry. "Labor that does not spring out of worship," he would admonish, "is futile and can only be wood, hay, and stubble in the day that shall try every man's work."

Rebelling against the hectic schedules that kept his fellow ministers and fellow Christians from true worship, Tozer wrote, "I am convinced that the dearth of great saints in these times, even among those who truly believe in Christ, is due at least in part to our unwillingness to give sufficient time to the cultivation of the knowledge of God. Our religious activities should be ordered in such a way as to leave plenty of time for the cultivation of the fruits of solitude and silence."

Tozer was an ardent lover of hymns and had in his library a collection of old hymnals. Often on his way to an appointment, he would meditate on one of the old hymns.

"Get a hymnbook," he frequently advised when counseling others, "but don't get one that is less than a hundred years old!" His Chicago church did not use the denomination's *Hymns of the Christian Life*. Instead, the congregation sang from a River Brethren Church hymnal. Tozer preferred this particular hymnal because it contained more of the great hymns he so loved, and he enjoyed hearing his people sing them.

"After the Bible," he said in an *Alliance Life* article aimed at new Christians, "the next most valuable book is a good hymnal. Let any new Christian spend a year prayerfully meditating on the hymns of Watts and Wesley alone, and he or she will become a fine theologian." Then he added, "Afterward, let that person read a balanced diet of the Puritans and the Christian mystics. The result will be more wonderful than he could have dreamed." This was his personal pattern, year after year.

During the 1950s, Tozer found a kindred spirit in a plumber from Ireland, Tom Haire, a lay preacher. Haire became the subject of seven articles Tozer wrote for *Alliance Life* entitled "The Praying Plumber from Lisburn," later reissued as a booklet. Two men could hardly have been more different, yet their love for God and their sense of His worth drew them together.

Once, while Haire was visiting Chicago, Tozer's church was engaged in a night of fasting and prayer. Haire joined them. In the middle of the night, he got thirsty and went out for a cup of tea. Some church members felt that Tom, by doing so, had "yielded to the flesh." Tozer disagreed. He saw in that act the beautiful liberty Tom enjoyed in the Lord.

Just before Haire was to return to his homeland, he stopped by Chicago to say good-bye.

"Well, Tom," Tozer remarked, "I guess you'll be going back to Ireland to preach."

"No," Tom replied in his thick Irish brogue. "I intend to cancel all appointments for the next six months and spend that time preparing for the Judgment Seat of Christ while I can still do something about it." It was an attitude not uncharacteristic of Tozer himself.

Tozer-grams

- If one-tenth of one percent of the prayers made in any American city on any Sabbath day were answered, the world would see its greatest revival come with the speed of light. We seem to have gotten used to prayers that produce nothing. God still hears prayer, and all His promises are still good, yet we go on at a pretty dying rate. Can someone tell us the answer for this?

- I had been naïve enough to believe that we had been disillusioned by the sorry performances of the personality boys of a few years ago, and that we had recovered from that form of abnormal psychology that we caught from the movies, but evidently I was too optimistic. Like malaria, it's back on us again.

• The first work of revealed truth is to secure an unconditional surrender of the sinner to the will of God. Until this has been accomplished, nothing really lasting has been done at all. The reader may admire the rich imagery of the Bible, its bold figures, and impassioned flights of eloquence; he may enjoy its tender musical passages and revel in its strong homely wisdom, but until he has submitted to its full authority over his life, he has secured no good from it yet.

O God, I have tasted Thy goodness, and it has both satisfied me and made me thirsty for more. I am painfully conscious of my need of further grace. I am ashamed of my lack of desire. O God, the Triune God, I want to want Thee; I long to be filled with longing; I thirst to be made more thirsty still. Show me Thy glory, I pray Thee, so that I may know Thee indeed. Begin in mercy a new work of love within me. Say to my soul, "Rise up, my love, my fair one, and come away." Then give me grace to rise and follow Thee up from this misty lowland where I have wandered so long. In Jesus' name, amen.

A.W. Tozer (1897–1963) was a self-taught theologian, pastor, and writer whose powerful words continue to grip the intellect and stir the soul of today's believer. He authored more than forty books. *The Pursuit of God* and *The Knowledge of the Holy* are considered modern devotional classics. Get Tozer information and quotes at twitter.com/TozerAW.

Reverend James L. Snyder is an award–winning author whose writings have appeared in more than eighty periodicals and fifteen books. He is recognized as an authority on the life and ministry of A.W. Tozer. His first book, *The Life of A.W. Tozer: In Pursuit of God*, won the Readers' Choice Award in 1992 by *Christianity Today*. Because of his thorough knowledge of Tozer, James was given the rights from the A.W. Tozer estate to produce new books derived from over four hundred never-before-published audiotapes. James and his wife live in Ocala, Florida. Learn more at awtozerclassics.com, or contact James at jamessnyder51@gmail.com.

More from A.W. Tozer and James L. Snyder

The truth and revelation that underpin Tozer's writings continue to inspire Christ followers today. This 365-day devotional will help you strengthen your daily walk with God. Each devotion includes a passage of Scripture, a short reading from Tozer, and a prayer. You will be drawn to truer worship, greater faith, deeper prayer, and more passion for Christ.

My Daily Pursuit

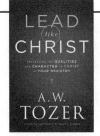

As a Christian, does your leadership approach look any different from that of those who don't follow Christ? Rather than focusing on the nuts and bolts of management, *Lead like Christ* looks closely at how leaders can imitate the greatest Leader of all. This step of humility and obedience will result in powerful, long-lasting change in your leadership role.

Lead like Christ

Many believe that God is everywhere but have yet to experience His presence. Using the story of Moses and the burning bush, Tozer teaches how proper worship has to be equal to the One we are worshiping; this means having a spirit of reverence and holiness. Let this book teach you how to kneel and worship before God's holy fire.

The Fire of God's Presence

BETHANYHOUSE

Stay up to date on your favorite books and authors with our free e-newsletters. Sign up today at bethanyhouse.com.

 facebook.com/BHPnonfiction

 @bethany_house

@bethany_house_nonfiction